Contents

Foreword by Martin Glenn

Why do we need another book on leadership? If there is one area of management that is not short of advice from all quarters, it is leadership skills. There are hundreds of thousands of leadership titles in circulation at any one time – put 'leadership books' into an internet search engine and you will get over a quarter of a million hits. But if there are so many good books available on leadership, why are so many of today's leaders still not up to the job?

The vast majority of leadership books fall into one of two categories, which, in my view, is why so many fail. The first category is what I would call quasi-academic, approaching the subject from too academic a standpoint and trying to force the facts of practical leadership into a unifying theory. The second is the leadership memoir which, with some exceptions, is often little more than congratulatory self-justification.

Anyone who has found themselves in any form of leadership role – which, I would argue, covers anyone who has raised a child through to the chief executive of a multinational corporation – knows that leadership is a life skill. It is a craft and not a science. How do people develop good craft skills? While some of the basic principles can be taught in the classroom, ultimately you learn through observation, emulation and practice. That is why this book is so necessary.

In putting together this book, the authors have asked craftsman's questions. They have observed and questioned and while they look for commonalities in the leadership approach of this diverse collection of leaders, they are never distracted by the need to fit all of the observations into neat conclusions.

I imagine that all of the leaders who were interviewed for this book found it an extremely useful experience. I know I did. It is inevitable that, given our busy lives, few of us have ever taken the time to think through and analyse what we do every day. For me as a leader, sitting down and thinking carefully about the things that drive my own approach to leadership was a valuable process.

The results of the research in this book should also provide anyone in a position of responsibility with the opportunity to engage in the leadership debate on an entirely different level. It offers great condensed learnings and the views and experiences of a wonderfully eclectic mix of people from a wide variety of fields. Above all, their experiences show clearly that every leader is different and that the best recognize their strengths and weaknesses and adapt their leadership style accordingly.

There is no single, magical recipe for successful leadership. The best leaders have a portfolio of styles and skills and the instinct to know when to use them. Good leadership means knowing when the time is right to change gear.

Introduction

The world of management has, in the words of *Financial Times* journalist Richard Donkin, a fixation on leadership that borders on obsession. But the business world is not alone in its fascination. On any given day the media surrounds us with stories of outstanding, indifferent or poor leadership in sport, politics, education, the military and any other number of situations.

Leaders are inevitably praised when things go right and invariably vilified when things go wrong. Everything, it seems, from sporting success to the collapse of a society, can be traced back to good or bad leadership. It is hardly surprising then, that we have developed an obsession with what it takes to be a successful leader. *Fortune* magazine, in identifying America's most admired companies, made the point that there is no one determining factor that makes a company admirable. But, if forced to search for an answer, most people would plump for leadership. As the American financier and businessman Warren Buffet once said, 'People are voting for the artist and not the painting.'

Management literature is rife with theories about the essential qualities of an effective leader. Equally numerous are the theories of what leadership actually *means.* These vary from the infuriatingly vague ('Managers are people who do things right; leaders are people who do the right thing') to the straightforwardly simplistic ('Leaders press for change').

It seems that today's leaders need to meet an ever-growing list of skills and personal characteristics in order to be considered effective. Inevitably this list will include words such as 'passion', 'commitment', 'vision' and that most elusive of all, 'charisma'. But, as Professor Brian Morgan of the University of Wales Institute School argues, 'despite the ease with which these characteristics are listed in textbooks, in practice things are not quite this simple. There is no consistent list of descriptors that can help us identify outstanding leaders.'

Leadership may be an elusive concept but surely it cannot be that mysterious. After all, many people do it every day, in every walk of life.

This led us to ask, but what do leaders *really* do? How many of today's leaders match up to the academic ideal? Does their behaviour as leaders correspond in any way to the various leadership models and theories? Do their everyday actions conform, consciously or unconsciously, to the predetermined standards we set for them? Do any of them take any notice of what a leader 'should' be?

Our research has been heavily influenced by writers who have concentrated on practical observation of leadership, such as John Kotter, and by the work of Rob Goffee and Gareth Jones, authors of *Why Should Anyone Be Led By You?*, who argue that the best leaders are 'authentic chameleons' who adapt their behaviour according to circumstances, but remain true to themselves throughout. This view is born from our discussions with the leaders in this book. Each had different personalities and different strengths and weaknesses but had learned, generally through trial and error, how to get the best out of their people and their organization.

The results of our research are a fascinating insight into the minds of a set of leaders from a wide range of fields. What struck us the most was how many of these people were instinctive leaders, with little or no formal training and very little reference to any form of leadership thought or literature. They just did what they felt was right. Some even found it difficult to accept what they do as leadership, as Sebastian Coe told us: 'I never, ever think of myself as a leader. I just do what I do.'

Others modestly take the view that their role is unimportant as long as the organization is functioning well. Gail Rebuck of Random House says, rather disarmingly, that she 'doesn't do anything' as a leader. 'My job is only to think and occasionally act as trouble shooter.' The rugby player Martin Johnson echoes this view: 'Being captain is almost like a managing director's role. If the team is working well you don't really need to do anything much.'

Effective leaders, in other words, are able to get their organization to a position where it is able to run smoothly with the minimum of intervention from the top. Dame Stella Rimington, who was the first female director-general of MI5, puts this view very clearly:

> *'There are actually very few things, if you analyse and put them all into boxes, that a leader does. But from the leader flows everything. He or she dictates the culture of the organization and its direction. Leadership also means looking ahead to see where the next challenge is coming from. And that, actually, is all you have to do.'*

These leaders recognize, though, that with success comes the danger of complacency. As Ron Dennis, the chairman and CEO of McLaren says, 'the biggest barrier to continued success, is continued success'. A good leader is constantly pushing their organization and their people to be the best that they can be. Charles Dunstone, CEO of the Carphone Warehouse told us that he saw his main role as leader of the company as 'to be unreasonable':

> *'Big organizations tend to become more and more reasonable as they grow. The IT project may run £2 million over budget and may*

be eight weeks late on delivery, but the view is that everyone will be paid so it's not the end of the world. That's not good enough. I'm not a tyrant but I try to push the business to do better than it thinks it can and never to take the easy option. I love the quote that Roger Bannister gave when he ran the four-minute mile when he was asked how he had managed to do it. He said that it was about the ability to take more out of yourself than you have got to give. That's what you try to do as the leader of a business.'

Above all, the leaders we spoke to all have a common characteristic: an unbridled passion for what they do. 'I know what I want. I want to make a difference in sport,' Sue Campbell, the chair of UK Sport told us. 'I want to make a difference in a world that I understand, and which has made a difference for me.'

ACKNOWLEDGEMENTS

We could not have written this book without the help of many people. Particular thanks go to Gareth Jones, Fellow of the Centre for Management Development at London Business School and co-author of *Why Should Anyone Be Led by You?*, and Professor Graham Jones, co-founder of the business consultancy Lane 4, who both provided invaluable guidance during our research, and Professor Brian Morgan, director of the Creative Leadership and Enterprise Centre at the University of Wales Institute, Cardiff.

We would also like to thank the 17 leaders who provided their time and support in sharing their experiences of leadership for the book:

- **Sue Campbell CBE** was appointed Reform Chair of UK Sport in September 2003 and confirmed as chair of the high-performance sports agency for a four-year term in March 2005. A former member of the England women's netball team and manager of the England women's basketball team, she was chief executive of the National Coaching Foundation between 1985 and 1995 and chief executive of The Youth Sport Trust between 1995 and 2005. Sue was elected chair of the Youth Sport Trust in 2005.

- **Sebastian Coe (Baron Coe)** is chairman of the London Organising Committee of the Olympic Games and the Paralympic Games. During his career as an athlete he set 12 world records and won 11 gold medals at major championships, including two Olympic golds. On his retirement from athletics, he was elected a Conservative MP and was Private Secretary to William Hague. He was appointed chairman of the London 2012 Olympic Games and Paralympic Games Bid Committee in 2004.
- **Nasser Hussain** was captain of the England cricket team for 45 test matches between 1999 and 2003.
- **Martin Johnson CBE** led the England rugby team to its historic World Cup win in 2003. While he was captain of the Leicester Tigers, the team won back-to-back Heineken Cup victories and won the league six times. He was named captain of England in 1998 and has captained the British Lions on two separate tours.
- **Sir Clive Woodward OBE** coached the England rugby team to its World Cup win in Australia in 2003. During his rugby career he played for Leicester Tigers, gained 21 caps for England and toured twice with the British Lions, while also forging a successful career at Rank Xerox and later launching his own leasing business. He was appointed coach to the England team in 1997 and was head coach for the British Lions tour to New Zealand in 2005. In 2006 he was appointed Director of Elite Performance at the British Olympic Association.
- **Charles Dunstone** founded, with David Ross, the mobile phone retailer Carphone Warehouse in 1989 and is chief executive of the multinational company.
- **Ron Dennis CBE** is chairman and chief executive of the McLaren Group and principal of the Vodafone McLaren Mercedes Formula One team. Dennis was chief mechanic to Sir Jack Brabham before launching his own racing team in the 1970s. The company's merger with Team McLaren marked the beginning of a highly successful racing career, including seven constructors' and nine drivers' world championships.
- **Greg Dyke** was director-general of the BBC between 2000 and 2004, when he resigned in the wake of the Hutton Inquiry. He

started his broadcasting career in London Weekend Television before moving to TV-am, where he was instrumental in reviving the show's ratings. He was appointed director of programmes at TVS before returning to LWT before its acquisition by Granada.

- **Martin Glenn** was appointed CEO of the Birds Eye Iglo Group in November 2006. A marketing specialist, he joined Walkers Snack Foods in 1992, becoming president in 1998, before becoming President of PepsiCo UK, one of the UK's leading soft drinks and snack food manufacturers, in 2003.

- **Heather Rabbatts CBE** worked as a barrister before moving into local government. She was chief executive of the London Borough of Merton before rising to prominence as chief executive of the London Borough of Lambeth authority between 1995 and 2000. On leaving Lambeth she founded and was chief executive of iMPower, a public sector consultancy, and was later managing director of 4Learning, Channel 4's education programmes and business. Rabbatts was appointed executive deputy chair of Millwall FC in May 2006 and executive chair of Millwall Holdings plc in October 2006. She is a former governor of the BBC, and current non executive director of the Bank of England and of the UK Film Council.

- **Gail Rebuck CBE** is chair and chief executive of Random House, one of the UK's leading trade publishing companies with over 40 imprints and publisher of many of the world's best known authors. She was founder director of Century Publishing, which merged with Hutchinson in 1985 before being acquired by Random House Inc. in 1989 and Bertelsmann in 1998. She was a member of the government's Creative Industries Task Force and is currently a Trustee of the Work Foundation, a member of the Council of the Royal College of Art and a non executive director of BSkyB.

- **Kevin Roberts** is worldwide chief executive of Saatchi & Saatchi. Born in Lancaster, he began his career as brand director to Mary Quant in the 1960s, before moving on to Gillette, Procter & Gamble and Pepsi Cola. He was chief operating officer at Lion Nathan Breweries in New Zealand before joining Saatchi & Saatchi in 1997. He is CEO in residence at The Judge Business

School at Cambridge University and chairman of the USA rugby board.

- **Dame Stella Rimington** was director-general of MI5 between 1992 and 1996. She was the first head of the service to be named publicly on her appointment and during her tenure she oversaw a new policy of openness at the service. She joined MI5 in India in 1967 and during her career worked in counter-espionage, counter-subversion and counter-terrorism. She was appointed to one of two deputy director-general positions in 1990.

- **Major General Patrick Cordingley** commanded the 7th Armoured Brigade Group (the Desert Rats) during the first Gulf War in 1991. He was awarded the Distinguished Service Order for his courage and leadership.

- **Field Marshal Peter Inge (Lord Inge)** was chief of the general staff between 1992 and 1994. He became chief of defence staff in 1994 until his retirement in 1997. During his army career he was Commanding Officer of the 1st Battalion of the Green Howards, serving in Northern Ireland and Germany. He was Director General, Logistics Policy at the Ministry of Defence and Commander of NATO's Northern Army Group. He became a privy councillor in 2004 and was a member of the Butler Committee.

- **Colonel Bob Stewart DSO** commanded the 1st Battalion of the Cheshire Regiment and was the first British Commander under UN command in Bosnia between 1992 and 1993. He was awarded the Distinguished Service Order and later became Chief of Policy at Supreme Headquarters Allied Powers Europe.

- **Commander Nigel 'Sharkey' Ward DSC AFC** commanded the 801 Naval Air Squadron (based in HMS Invincible) during the Falklands War in 1982 and was senior Sea Harrier adviser to the Command on the tactics, direction and progress of the air war. He flew over 60 war missions, shot down three enemy aircraft and was later awarded the Distinguished Service Cross for gallantry.

PART ONE

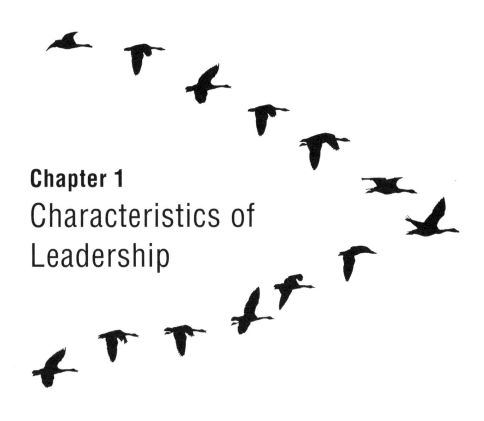

Chapter 1
Characteristics of Leadership

I have no special gift. I am only passionately curious.

Albert Einstein

What does it take to be a leader? What skills, strengths and personality traits do you need? Leadership literature is certainly not shy on suggestions – and you can guarantee that words such as 'charisma', 'determination', 'commitment', 'passion' and 'vision' will crop up frequently. But, as Brian Morgan of Cardiff Business School points out, in practice things are never that simple. 'There is no consistent list of descriptors that will help us identify outstanding leaders,' he says. Morgan quotes the views of the business theorist Peter Drucker on entrepreneurs: 'Some are eccentrics, others conformists; … some are worriers, some relaxed; … some drink quite heavily, some are total abstainers; ... some are people of great charm and warmth ... some have no more personality than a frozen mackerel.'

Drucker's entertaining observation is equally true of leaders. As Martin Glenn says, there is no right or wrong way to lead, there are just different ways.

'When I first got into management I used to think about the right way to behave and I think that came from a lack of self-confidence. The conclusion I've come to over the years is not that anything goes, but that there are a vast variety of effective leadership styles. There is no cookie cutter for leadership.'

Goffee and Jones agree with this view: 'Books on leadership persistently try to find a recipe for leadership,' they write.[1] 'Beleaguered executives are invited to compare themselves with lists of leadership competences and characteristics – against which they always find themselves wanting ... In our view, there are no universal leadership characteristics. What works for one leader will not work for another.'

The leaders we spoke to would agree. All had contrasting views about the characteristics that make for a great or successful leader. Honesty, integrity and moral courage were words that cropped up frequently. As Charles Dunstone, chief executive and co-founder of the Carphone Warehouse puts it: 'There's quite a lot of bullshit written about leadership but at its core, leadership is about integrity. If people believe in you and what you are trying to do, they will follow you. If they don't, they won't.'

Leaders consistently make the point that they can form a clear vision and have all the skills necessary to communicate their plans throughout the organization, but they will get nowhere unless people recognize that they believe in what they are doing. 'Underpinning everything is your values, it is what drives you,' says Sue Campbell, chair of UK Sport. 'Your sense of fairness and honesty.'

This viewpoint reappears over and over, irrespective of the field in which the leaders operate. Nasser Hussain, who captained the England cricket team between 1999 and 2003, says that honesty is 'absolutely key' to good leadership. 'Players have to believe in you and trust you in order to play for you. Michael Atherton [who captained the side when Hussain first joined the team] was as honest as anything and I would have played for him forever.' Military leaders make this point most forcefully, saying that morale is the first thing to suffer if soldiers are not convinced that their cause is right and that their leaders are fully committed to it. 'It's terribly important that you believe in what you are doing and what you are asking your people to do,' says Major General Patrick Cordingley. Field Marshal Lord Inge agrees, saying that the soldiers have to trust in the ability of their commander and in his belief in them. They also have to trust that in the event of war, the leader will not put their lives unnecessarily at risk. Kevin Roberts, the worldwide CEO of Saatchi & Saatchi, describes the business world equivalent as 'loyalty beyond reason'.

Closely linked to this need for integrity and belief in the shared vision of the organization, is passion. 'You need to have passion about you,' says Nasser Hussain. 'That might mean wearing your heart on your sleeve, as I did, or having an iron fist in a velvet glove, which is the Michael Vaughan way. Outwardly he is smiling but inwardly he has a great passion to make things happen.' Gail Rebuck of Random House says that '100% commitment to the organization is absolutely essential; a passion for what you are doing'. Lord Inge characterizes this phenomenon of good leaders simply as 'love' for their organization:

'When I left the army I joined the board of Racal Electronics, which was run by a remarkable man called Ernie [Sir Ernest] Harrison. He loved Racal. I think he was the 15th employee ever to join the company, and he clearly loved it. As well as having a detailed knowledge of how the City worked, how the products worked and how the organization worked, he clearly loved Racal and I think that's very important. If someone is in a company only to make money, it won't be a great comfort to anyone who works there.'

One of the most challenging aspects of leadership for many people is striking the right balance between making decisions as a leader and encouraging a creative atmosphere in an organization where innovation and ideas can develop. Inevitably, this will involve developing a working environment where people feel able to question and challenge decisions. 'Leadership is about not taking yourself too seriously, in my view,' says Colonel Bob Stewart. 'It means understanding that even the most humble person can help you, and can lead too.'

Colonel Stewart tells of the advice his father, a Royal Air Force officer, gave him when he was about to enter Sandhurst for officer training at the age of 17.

'I was terrified about what I was about to go through and overawed by everything I saw. As I approached the Grand Entrance Dad said to me, "Remember, Robert, the Queen gets diarrhoea and always looks downwards before you look up". That's leadership in one sentence, in my view. It describes how an officer and a leader should behave. You engender enthusiasm, confidence and trust by clearly backing your subordinates.'

Many leaders make the point that one of the fundamental requirements of a good leader is that he or she is good at the underlying job, and not just at leadership itself. Major General Patrick Cordingley makes the point that even if a leader is not actually doing what he is asking his followers to do, it stands to reason that he has to understand exactly what he is asking of them.

'It sounds ridiculous but if you are a brigade commander of 150 armoured tanks, you have to know how they work. You will have an adviser alongside you but you still have to be an expert in the range of the guns and how they fire. And when you come to a minefield and a sapper tells you that it is 100 yards wide and looks as though it has anti-tank mines, you have to know how you get through it. You have to have all of that knowledge, you really do.'

The fighter pilot, Sharkey Ward, adds that it is vital, in his sphere, to be good at the job. 'You can still be a leader if you're not, but it makes life a whole lot easier if you are top notch.'

Sporting captains are, of course, on the field because of the quality of their own playing talents. Nasser Hussain says that he was told by the selectors after being appointed captain to make sure that he looked after his own game. 'There's nothing better than having your leader out there, fighting from the front and getting runs himself,' he says.

Decision-making lies at the heart of any leader's role (Ron Dennis, chief executive of McLaren, argues that taking decisions is the leader's primary function). Martin Glenn believes that this demands the clarity of thought that characterizes a good leader. 'It is possible to have leadership in chaos but it's hardly ideal,' he says. 'You have to be able to simplify complex situations so you can create a hierarchy of things that are important.' Dame Stella Rimington, the former head of MI5, agrees: 'You do need a clear mind. One of the dangers of being a leader is that you can get cluttered up with things. You have to be able to sort out the important stuff with clarity from everything that is coming at you.' Keeping sight of this vision while an organization copes with the change that inevitably goes on around and within it is a constant challenge for today's leaders, demanding flexibility and foresight as well as a steely resolve and a willingness to take risks. It is also why leaders can be in a painfully lonely position.

John Kotter argues that while management is about coping with complexity, leadership is about coping with change. 'Management is about doing things right. Management is survival,' agrees Kevin Roberts of Saatchi & Saatchi. 'If all you do is management, you will survive but that does not provide competitive advantage in today's environment.'

The distinction between management and leadership is a key issue in understanding what makes a good leader. According to Professor Brian Morgan of the University of Wales Institute, leadership and management are different and distinctive but they share some complementary skills. Both are necessary to run complex organizations but the key difference is that management is about planning, co-ordinating and putting appropriate performance systems in place. Leadership, on the other hand, is about being visionary, proactive and anticipating change – or even responding positively to change. Managers can be inspirational but leaders create the capacity for people to do something different – to do more than they would normally do.

These skills are harder to pin down and the leaders we spoke to put forward a number of different theories. 'A leader has to have perspective on the business, and has to be able to see around corners,' says Martin Glenn. 'A leader also should be able to challenge convention and be open-minded and creative. Should you always take rules literally?' Colonel Bob Stewart agrees that leadership is about 'challenging the status quo. Don't just accept the rules. If the rules say it can't be done, bend them or change them. A leader is someone who makes things happen and takes risks.'

It is an interesting reflection of the more 'modern' style of leadership that is prevalent today – empathetic and authentic leadership, rather than the command and control model – that many of the leaders identified emotional skills as one of their key characteristics of leadership. 'I think leadership is more about emotion than it is about logic,' is the view of Field Marshal Lord Inge. 'If you can get hold of a man's or woman's emotions, you have the key. All the great leaders have this gift.'

'The classic statement is that you can't lead unless people follow so you have to have that ability to understand what makes the people around you tick,' says Dame Stella Rimington. 'I think it goes back to genuinely listening and trying to understand what is really going on, and then moulding that into something that will take you in the direction you need to be going.'

The leaders who naturally adopt an empathetic style of leadership – most notably Greg Dyke, the former director-general of the BBC – say that it seems obvious to them that employees who are respected, trusted and treated well will perform to the best of their ability.

'I don't do detail, I never have done, and I have the concentration levels of a peanut so I am very happy to just believe that people will come up with the results if you let them get on with it.'

Sir Clive Woodward, who coached the World Cup-winning England rugby team, believes that people develop respect for a leader that cares about them and their well-being.

'You can't demand respect, you earn it through the quality of your actions. There's no shortcut. Leadership is about respect and it comes from the quality of what you do and how you conduct yourself.

It comes from taking an interest in each individual person and helping them improve.'

The military leader Colonel Bob Stewart echoes this view:

'The first principle of an officer is that you lead by example and care for the people below you. I learned when I was a platoon commander that the key is to get the respect of the soldiers. Little things matter, like visiting them if they are ill. You don't need a pip or a star on your shoulder in order to lead. You want people to follow you because they wish to do so.'

Greg Dyke adds that effective leadership can only happen when the leader is not only respected but loved within the organization:

'I came across someone recently from the London Business School who had been teaching leadership for years. She said she had always taught that you don't need to be loved as a leader but you do need to be respected. But over the past five years she has changed her mind. She now says that the only way you can move and change organizations is if you are loved. Bill Gates is loved. Phil Knight of Nike is loved. Jack Walsh was tough when he was at GE – he got rid of about 10% of the workforce a year for a while – but the people who were left loved him. I would really like to go and talk to the people at Marks & Spencer about Stuart Rose. I suspect that they love him because he saved them. They had spent the previous 10 years being told the organization was rubbish and suddenly they are good again.'

There are many other characteristics that make for a successful leader. Heather Rabbatts, who became chief executive of Lambeth Council after replying to a job advertisement for 'possibly the worst job in local government', understandably says that leaders should be willing to take personal risks:

'You have to be brave. I couldn't go to Lambeth and not be brave, so I think you do need strength of character and resilience. I am quite driven and I want to see things work. I'm like an adrenaline junkie. The more pressure you put me under, the better I am.'

The one element that is completely out of control of leaders, though, is luck, both in terms of their journey up the leadership ladder and in terms of their career at the top. 'There is a story about Napoleon being presented with several candidates for promotion to General,' says Colonel Bob Stewart. 'All of them knew their trade and were outstanding leaders. And Napoleon said that they were all clearly good candidates. But he asked which of them was lucky!'

THE CHARISMA QUESTION

John F Kennedy had it and Bill Clinton has a great deal of it. So, on the other hand, did Hitler. Charisma – variously defined as extreme charm and grace, or a magnetic quality, or an uncanny ability to charm or influence followers – is a source of endless debate in the field of leadership. Do leaders need it? Can you be an effective leader without it?

In a command and control model, a charismatic leader is not strictly necessary. In a leadership model that depends on inspiring and persuading employees to follow, it can be a positive bonus. That said, an overly charismatic leader can occasionally hide some deep-rooted problems within an organization, as the pensioners of Robert Maxwell's Mirror Group will testify. Some organizations perform poorly with a charismatic leader, others perform mercurially with a leader that has, as Peter Drucker puts it, the personality of a frozen fish.

Some of the leaders we spoke to have that quality that could be defined as charisma – Kevin Roberts, Sue Campbell, Heather Rabbatts and Sharkey Ward would certainly fall into that category. Others have more 'quiet' personalities but are nevertheless strong and effective leaders.

It is possible to fake charisma and many leaders agree that there is an element of conscious drama to their role, and that at times they must 'act' as leaders. Unsurprisingly, the leaders we spoke to are split on whether charisma is a necessary quality for leadership. Sir Clive Woodward does not believe that charisma is necessary at all:

'Leadership is about respect, not charisma. I see charisma as meaning that the leader has a charismatic personality or a high profile and I don't think you need that. There are people out there who are nothing like that who are still outstanding leaders.'

Heather Rabbatts agrees, but adds that she used to believe that charisma was important in leadership.

'I have met people since then who are not personally charismatic but who are very effective. There are people, and I would include Greg Dyke among them, who, when they walk into the room, the atmosphere changes. And there are others, such as [Tesco chief executive] Terry Leahy, whom you wouldn't immediately notice had walked into the room. Yet he is clearly a very talented leader and whenever I hear him talk he is insightful and interesting. So I don't think it's a requirement, but it makes a difference. If you have some presence and charisma it helps you to win people over. You don't need to work quite so hard at motivating them.'

'You have to have an ability to take people with you – some people have that and some don't,' says Charles Dunstone of Carphone Warehouse. 'I remember talking to somebody about [the former Prime Minister] John Major, and they said to me that if you met him in private he was the most fantastically interesting and charismatic man. I guess that he would have to be because you don't get to be Prime Minister if you don't have that quality. But somehow he could never get that across publicly and that was ultimately his undoing.'

Sebastian Coe, who is a former MP and adviser to the former leader of the opposition William Hague, says that the charisma and charm of Tony Blair was a huge asset during the final bidding process for the Olympic and Paralympic Games in Singapore in 2005:

'Some people just have that presence and fill a room as soon as they walk into it, and he has that. We all know plenty of people in all walks of life that can be funny and amusing around a dinner table but when you put them behind a microphone, it doesn't work. It's a huge asset to have presence in politics. Because of the television age it's almost a dealbreaker if you don't have it. I don't think charisma is a luxurious add-on. You can't lead people unless you excite them.'

Sue Campbell of UK Sport agrees that charisma is extremely helpful as a leadership trait but argues that there is a clear difference between an extrovert personality and charisma. 'If you are in the presence of Nelson Mandela he doesn't gabble on but he is instantly charismatic in a soft way. You do need to have a certain kind of presence where people get a sense of who you are and what you are about. I think that comes from an inner confidence rather than anything else.'

Dame Stella Rimington agrees with this point:

'There are the kind of leaders, which I am not, who can come into an organization convinced about what they want to do and who carry it through by the sheer force of their personality. That's all very well, wowing everyone with your charisma, but in the long term the people have to buy into what you are persuading them to do. They might initially do that but in the end doubts will begin to creep in if the plan does not have a firm basis. That said, I think charisma is important because people have got to want to follow you and they tend to follow people who have that ability to express themselves and convince people.'

Dame Stella's point, that ultimately what matters is that people believe that the leader is right, is a recurring theme. Gail Rebuck of Random House argues that people tend to respond to leaders who show themselves as they are, vulnerabilities and all. 'If you do that I think you can develop a presence that people are willing to follow,' she says. Martin Glenn touches on the point that there is a fine line between charisma and megalomania. 'Anyone who has a massive ego will start off by being less effective as a leader unless it is counteracted by some form of brilliance,' he says. 'I've had one or two bosses like that, with egos the size of a planet, but brilliant. They can just about pull it off but what they don't do is lay down the tracks for the future people to build upon. Their legacy tends to be about how good they were in the current situation.'

A SUBSTITUTE FOR CHARISMA

If you are not fortunate enough to be born with the mystical quality of charisma, there are other options. Rob Goffee and Gareth Jones argue that one of the qualities of inspirational leaders is that they recognize and capitalize on what is unique about themselves. 'Often,' they say, 'a leader will show his differences by having a distinctly different dress style or physical appearance, but typically he will move on to distinguish himself through qualities like imagination, loyalty, expertise, or even a handshake. Anything can be a difference, but it is important to communicate it.'[2]

Jones and Goffee argue that inspirational leaders use these differences to deliberately signal their separateness from their followers, which in turn they use to motivate others to perform better. 'They recognize instinctively that followers will push themselves if their leader is just a little aloof,' they say. Some of the leaders we spoke to, however, make the more basic point that a quirky characteristic – anything from a distinctive personality trait to a handlebar moustache – simply makes them recognizable and easy to describe to others, which can be an invaluable attribute (particularly when leading a large organization). Richard Branson, head of Virgin, for instance, is easily recognized predominantly because he does not look or dress as you might expect the chief executive of a multinational company to appear.

In the armed forces, of course, the problems of recognizability are magnified by the fact that a leader is in charge of thousands of identically dressed soldiers. 'It's always quite helpful if the commander of a company or battalion has some affectionate but defining characteristic; maybe he speaks in a curious way,' says Major General Patrick Cordingley. 'As a commander you have to be known by your troops so it is quite useful to have some sort of feature.' Sharkey Ward adds that the Fleet Air Arm has a history of eccentric commanders. He cites one commander who always went to war with his favourite piece of literature in his pocket. 'It helps if you have a particular quality, or a certain something that endears you to the men, which in my case might be standing up to the more senior officers rather than being a "yes" man,' he says. 'I'm something of a legend because of this attitude. Getting things right has to come first. You couldn't really call it charisma.'

Other leaders have made the most of their own particular defining characteristics. Heather Rabbatts says that her Jamaican mother would be horrified to see her striking, long curly hair and flowing clothes:

'My mother would want to straighten my hair because that is what you do. I definitely get treated differently if I am in what I call my "corporate look" as opposed to more "me". It's something I'm certainly aware of, particularly at Millwall [Football Club]; because of the very white fan base I certainly stand out. I think that probably helps me in that environment.'

Kevin Roberts, the worldwide CEO of Saatchi & Saatchi is also well-known for always wearing a black t-shirt and trousers, whatever the occasion. His anti-establishment habits make him highly distinctive, although he says it all comes down to personal choice:

'I never wear a tie, not even if I'm seeing the board, and they all accept that. It's all OK as long as I continue to deliver. I won't go to a formal dinner if I have to wear a black tie. These choices are open to all of us most of the time. People compromise or follow their peers but I'm not big on that, and I don't expect it from other people either.'

LEADERSHIP BY OSMOSIS

The fact that no-one can agree on a definitive list of ingredients that makes for an effective leader illustrates how the understanding of leadership has changed in modern times. As John Kotter points out, the traditional view of leadership is based on the foundation that leadership is the province of a chosen few and that leaders are effectively born with the necessary skills. The organizational environment, however, has changed beyond recognition and continues to change at an alarming speed.

Kotter argues that twenty-first century organizations in the business world need to be dynamic and adaptive and this demands a different form of leadership. Leadership in the modern business world relies to a far greater extent on teamwork and encouraging leadership behaviour throughout the organization, he says.[3] This implies that more and more people are learning to develop leadership skills throughout their career.

Learning, of course, starts early but the best leaders continue to improve their skills throughout their lives. Most of this learning comes not from books but from observing the behaviour of others. In the following chapters we will look at how upbringing, education and people influence leaders and the way they behave.

WHAT LEADERS REALLY DO

Leaders believe that:

- At its core, leadership is about integrity
- Trust should move in both directions
- Good leaders are rarely poor at their underlying job
- Clarity of thought is an essential skill for leaders
- Leadership is more about emotion than it is about logic
- Leaders should lead by example, not direction
- Luck inevitably plays a part in anyone's career
- Being different helps to set a leader apart and makes them easily identifiable.
- Leaders should set a clear direction.

---

[1] *Why Should Anyone Be Led by You?*, p10
[2] *Why Should Anyone Be Led By You?,* Harvard Business Review, September-October 2000, p 69
[3] *Leading Change*, p 175

Chapter 2
Background

No leader sets out to be a leader. People set out to lead their lives, expressing themselves fully. When that expression is of value, they become leaders.

Warren Bennis

Are leaders born, or made? It is a question that is invariably raised in any discussion of leadership and has yet to be answered. Are some people born with the magical ability to persuade people to follow them? Or are the skills subconsciously learned during their early years? The view of the business writer Warren Bennis is that it is a 'dangerous myth' that leaders are born to lead. 'This myth asserts that people simply either have certain charismatic qualities or not.

That's nonsense: in fact, the opposite is true. Leaders are made rather than born.'

It is possible that leaders have some genetic advantage but the personality and character that are required to lead are invariably developed through a combination of early experiences, influences and opportunities. Later experiences in the educational system, at work and through role models and mentors also contribute to the collection of knowledge and skills that are necessary to lead well. Luck, too, often plays a part. Lord Inge argues that if someone has the spark of leadership within them, then education, training and experience can do a great deal to develop those qualities. Greg Dyke's view is that 10% of people are natural leaders, 10% could never lead anything and the remaining 80% could develop leadership skills with the right training.

Our leaders come from a wide range of backgrounds, the only common thread among them being the fact that they have, somehow, ended up in a leadership role. None can recall a burning desire to be a leader during their childhood and a high proportion feel that they ended up in a leadership role more by accident than by design. 'I don't think I've ever really thought of myself as a leader,' says Charles Dunstone of Carphone Warehouse. 'I'm a surprised leader, if you like. It wasn't something that I felt I was born to do or even felt very confident about.'

The leaders themselves have very different views on the subject of nature versus nurture. Greg Dyke argues that 'it doesn't matter about background, really. Some people just want to win and some don't.' He adds that, growing up in suburban London meant he was 'desperate not to be ordinary'. Ron Dennis, who set up his first car racing venture at the age of 25 and was in charge of McLaren at the age of 34, argues that future leaders have to have that elusive 'something' inside them 'but the question is whether it's self-taught or whether it's in the genes. Personally, I don't think it's genetic. History is full of politicians whose families have followed in their father's footsteps, and athletes who were children of athletes, but those that have succeeded probably just listened to their parents about what it takes to succeed.'

There are certainly cases where our leaders have followed in the footsteps of their parents, most prevalently with the military leaders. Colonel Bob Stewart says that, realistically, he had no choice on his career as the son of an air force officer (his colour blindness, though, meant he could not follow his father into the RAF). 'I was programmed to join the Army by my upbringing,' he says. 'I never, ever felt there was a decision to be made. The real problem I felt was whether I was good enough to pass officer selection.'

Major General Patrick Cordingley also came from a military family. 'No-one had really done anything else. Of course I started out wanting to be an engine driver when I was very young, but a career in the army was perfectly natural. No-one put any pressure on me but I never really thought of doing anything else.' He adds, though, that a military career was not necessarily thought of as a perilous choice at the time. 'This was during the Cold War. No-one actually thought they were ever going to fight.'

Some of our leaders remember a vague feeling of wanting to make an impact on the world. The former CEO of Pepsico, Martin Glenn, can recall 'an early sense of wanting to be noticed, or having a point of view that you want to test. It was really a question of wanting to know whether what I said would resonate with other people.' Sue Campbell, chair of UK Sport, had a similar experience:

'I had this sense of destiny since I was very young that I was going to change the future of sport. Goodness knows why, or how, and I had no idea what the journey would be, but I just had a sense of wanting to make a difference. Then each time I had an opportunity, I did the best I could and that somehow opened another door, and then another and another.'

Kevin Roberts, the worldwide CEO of Saatchi & Saatchi, believes that he is a product of his generation and that his career has been influenced strongly by the fact that he is one of the baby boomers:

'I'm very fortunate in that I am a product of my times. I was formed in the 1960s, when youth was given its head, and energized by

the technology of the 1990s. We were spiritually liberated in the 60s and people power is now with us again [in the 21ˢᵗ century]. The consumer is boss. But I have also been helped by the technology explosion because that has really liberated us. It has removed all constraints and barriers to liberation and innovation. There's nothing you can't do now. As Disney said, if you can dream it you can do it.'

Dame Stella Rimington, by contrast, reached a leadership role in spite of the expectations of her generation:

'I never set out wanting to lead anything and if anybody had suggested that to me I would have thought it was a very weird idea. I came from that generation of women who were expected to stop work when they got married and had children. That attitude was, in a sense, programmed into my mind. My early career was a question of doing the next job as well as I could, but also not wanting to work for anybody I felt was less competent than I was. I suppose I was thinking, "I can do that better than you," and convincing others that I could, and moving on to the next level.'

THE INFLUENCE OF FAMILY LIFE

It is clear that many of the leaders were born into extraordinary families, in the sense that they were surrounded with either a strong work ethic or were instilled with the belief that they could do whatever they wanted.

For the former England cricket captain Nasser Hussain, the family influences were partly cultural. 'A sense of family and respecting your elders is ingrained and it comes from being brought up in India and having an Indian father. We spoke when we were spoken to.'

The work ethic instilled in the young Essex schoolboy, though, went further than culture. The family – Nasser has two brothers and a sister – moved to England from India for the sake of the children's education and they were always aware that sacrifices had been made for them. That created an environment where the children were encouraged, but not pushed, to work hard:

'Academically, I was one year ahead of myself, not because I was bright but because private school was expensive and my dad sent all of us there even though he did not have much money. I always had to push myself because I was always 16th out of 18 in the class. If I had stayed in my year I might have been 5th in everything. And that's part of me now – everything I do I have to do properly.

'I also played at the cricket school in Ilford, which my dad ran. He was not what you might call a pushy dad but he was highly motivated. He had given up his lifestyle in India to bring us to England and it was costing him a lot of money, so we made sure that we made the most of it. It was a highly driven environment that we were in. It was a lot of fun and in the end it turned out well. It could have gone the other way.'

Gail Rebuck, now chief executive of the publishers Random House, grew up in a similarly driven environment. Her Jewish grandparents had fled to the UK before the war. 'My grandfather was a penniless, 15-year-old tailor when he arrived and had to make a living and build up his own business,' she explains. Her mother's family ran a greengrocer's business and both parents had to leave school early in order to support their families and the family business.

'That entrepreneurial spirit was just prevalent in my family. The discussions about when I would get my first job started when I was about 13. So I pretended I was 16 in order to get a Saturday job. The work ethic was very, very strong. And my mother had the memory of her working class background that drove her on to improve herself. She wanted her children to do better. I think that ethic was always there. You didn't complain. You just got on with things.'

Others of our leaders came from more unremarkable backgrounds. Martin Glenn describes his own home life as 'a wonderful, unromantically safe background' where both parents (who were schoolteachers) had reached significantly above the status they were born into. While the young Martin Glenn never felt he was pushed to achieve as a child, he recognizes that his stable and secure family environment allowed his confidence to grow.

Sue Campbell also says she owes a lot to 'a great mum and dad', particularly since both encouraged her to succeed even though she, in common with them, was not particularly academic. She admits that she was 'sporty, fiery and competitive' as a child but says that her subsequent success has come because she worked hard at everything even though she 'was never the best at anything I did by a long way. I just made the most of what I've got':

'I came from a home where I felt very secure. I wasn't a great success at school but I remember my father saying to me, "You will be whatever you want to be". And I believed him. They were both very supportive. Neither of them was good at school but my mother was a successful businesswoman and my father was very good with people. I'd say, using the modern language, that they both had very good emotional intelligence.

'My mother was a traditional mum. What mattered to her was that I was well-fed and healthy. When I first got on the England [netball] team, I remember ringing home in great excitement and she said, "Oh, that's nice dear. Will you be home for your tea?"'

EDUCATION

Schooling has played an important part in the lives of many of our leaders, for a variety of reasons. Kevin Roberts was one of the few to make a conscious decision to work as hard as possible at school in order to create a foundation for later life:

'Someone once said that the lack of alternatives focuses the mind. Well, I grew up in a typical working class small town in Lancashire and the lack of alternatives there did focus my mind. I knew I didn't want to spend my life there as one of the poor, oppressed working class. I had no financial way out and no way out through using any connections. The only way out was through education.'

Our leaders' experiences at the schools they attended – and they range from local comprehensives to private boarding schools – provide some insights into the impact an education system can have on a future leader. In particular, the leaders who came from an older generation (and particularly those educated in 'traditional' public schools) argue that the systems that were designed to single out pupils with leadership abilities (such as prefects and head boys and girls), many of which are now seen as unfashionable, played an important part in honing their leadership skills.

Sharkey Ward, who was captain of his school, says that he 'always looked up to the head of school and the prefects' as he was growing up. His own experience as captain of the school, he adds, was 'important leadership training, although mostly by trial and error'.

Major General Patrick Cordingley, who attended boarding school at Sherborne in the late 1950s, makes the point very clearly:

'People of my age were fortunate enough to go schools in which, although leadership was not actually taught, it was imbued in everything you did. The prefect system, the house system and the sports system was all about leadership and you had, at a reasonably young age, control over what younger boys were doing. It gave you a lot of confidence. Nowadays that's thought to be very dodgy. But nevertheless, it worked. It was abused, sadly, but you did learn about leadership. That spark of leadership is born in people and at the time I was being brought up, that was what this country was looking for. Those people who showed themselves to be skilful in leadership in some way went into leadership-orientated organizations, in my case the Armed Forces.'

For our leaders from a slightly younger generation, sport is a regular theme in developing their leadership skills at an early age. Nasser Hussain remembers competing fiercely with fellow pupils to be the best at cricket or football:

'I was constantly striving to be successful. There was a lad called Shepherd who opened the batting with me all through school. We used to get presented prizes in assembly – a cricket bat for scoring 100 runs or a ball for five wickets and it was always a target to be up there at the end of the week and have more than him at the end of the season.'

Grammar schools are singled out by our leaders as a significant influence on their early lives, although their influence is not always a direct one. In some cases, the experience of failing the 11-plus exam was eventually as formative as the experience of reaching a grammar school was for others.

Kevin Roberts, who grew up in Lancaster, considers the scholarship he gained to Lancaster Royal Grammar School to be one of the defining moments of his life. 'The grammar school system before Labour got a hold of it was a tremendous competitive advantage for working class kids like me,' he says. 'I was very fortunate. At school I was thrust into leadership roles very early on through sport. I was captain of the school rugby team from the age of 11 onwards.'

Greg Dyke passed his 11-plus exam and went to Hayes Grammar School, although he says he was 'a failure at school by the standards of academia'. He says in his autobiography *Inside Story*, though, that one of his most traumatic childhood memories was when his brother failed the 11-plus. 'It was a family tragedy and my parents were distraught. My hatred of the 11-plus, and the whole concept of selection at the age of 11, is rooted in those experiences.'

The experience of Martin Glenn, though, shows that failing the 11-plus did not necessarily doom a child to a life of underachievement. His sister and three brothers had all reached grammar school but he failed the 11-plus and was sent to the local Catholic comprehensive:

'My mum and dad were really worried but I think it was a great break. It was a time when there was plenty of money spent on schools and so the school environment felt significantly superior to our home environment – I don't think that's the case today. It was a very aspiring school. It was brand spanking new and the teachers wanted to achieve something. It was good.'

In Glenn's case, attending a comprehensive worked in his favour because he was able to stand out from the crowd; something that arguably would have been more difficult in a grammar school environment. The fact that he was good at sport was an added advantage as it meant he was singled out for leadership roles: 'I was seen as a boffin but was sporty enough for my intellectual competence to be justified. I was seen as down to earth yet clever so when there was a school committee I would typically be on that.' Sir Clive Woodward makes a similar point about his school, a 'small, tough boarding school':

'School was probably the biggest influence, in positive and negative terms. I was good at sport, and that set me apart from others. In sporting terms I was a long way beyond anyone else, whereas if I'd gone to a normal school there would probably have been kids there who were as good as or better than me.'

Martin Glenn also points out that, while he could have been in danger of being written off as a comprehensive school pupil, he was fortunate in that a teacher at his school encouraged him to take the Oxford entrance exam, which he passed. 'I was accepted to Merton College Oxford. I had no idea which college to choose. I still look back now and realize that was a massively lucky break. I felt in my first term that I was kidding myself and that I wasn't good enough. At every big promotion in my life that question has gone through my head.'

LEARNING LEADERSHIP

Aside from their experiences in various school teams and the military leaders who attended officer training at Sandhurst, very few of our leaders had anything that could be recognized as formal leadership training at any point. Most say that they learned through trial and error, on the job.

One of the exceptions is Greg Dyke, who attended the Advanced Management Programme at Harvard Business School in 1989, the year before he took over as managing director of LWT. He says that he had concerns about the course and was advised by his wife not to go, because she felt he was an instinctive leader and that intellectualizing the process could make him less effective.

The experience, in the event, did prove to be valuable. 'I was very fortunate to come across John Kotter, who lectured us twice a week,' says Dyke. 'He was the first person I'd come across who talked about the difference between management and leadership. It gave me an intellectual rationale for what I thought I did.' He adds in his autobiography that the biggest revelation 'was the discovery that the most successful organizations in the world were those that treated their staff properly. I believed in that concept but was surprised to discover it also led to competitive advantage.'

Patrick Cordingley attended Sandhurst for officer training, but says that at the time the college did not attempt to identify what specific leadership skills were required and none were specifically taught. The experience, though, did teach him the importance of team spirit:

'It certainly gave me a lot of confidence in my physical ability. And the second thing is that you made very good friends because you were all in this quite unpleasant training organization together and that made you bond. We realized that we worked very well as a team.'

CAREER PROGRESSION

Few of our leaders could claim to have a career plan with the ultimate aim of leadership in some form. For most, leadership was an accidental by-product of their talents, their drive, their beliefs and in some cases, was helped along by good fortune.

Gail Rebuck of Random House relates a typically chaotic early career, where she ended up in publishing almost by accident rather than by design:

> '*I was part of that generation that just assumed that I would come out of university and get a job, so it was a rude awakening when there wasn't a job to be had. I worked for a few months taking American high school students around Europe and then came back to London and worked as a driver for an independent antiques dealer. We opened an antiques stall on the King's Road, actually developed a really good business over four or five months but I remember sitting there one day, deciding on the mark-up for some piece of antique clothing and I suddenly thought, is this it? There must be more to life than this. So I took a six-week secretarial course. I went around the recruitment agencies and having earlier said I was under-qualified to work in an office, they told me I was over-qualified because although I could now type, I was a graduate and I would get bored by some of the menial tasks. But in the end I got a job with a children's book packager. The production director needed an assistant, which was even better than being called a secretary. The fact that I was hopeless at typing didn't seem to worry him very much.*'

Ron Dennis of McLaren says that during his early life he never saw himself as running a company. In his case, his engineering skills and entrepreneurial attitude meant that he would inevitably become a leader if his ideas were successful. 'It came really hand-in-hand with an entrepreneurial motion,' he says. 'When you start to see opportunity, you move towards the opening on your own but you quickly find out that you need to take people with you in order to be able to take advantage of that opportunity. And if you succeed, people believe that you have good judgement and agree with the direction in which you're going. And you become the leader.'

Nasser Hussain argues that he ended up as captain of the England team not because he was a great player – technically, he says, he was poor at cricket – but because he was interested in tactics. 'I was a watcher. I'm a firm believer that you learn a lot by watching. Because of that I learned a lot about the game and I think that was a plus when it came to being captain.' As for his career, he says he was never aiming to be captain of the national side. In common with Stella Rimington, whose initial aim was only to do 'the next job' as well as she could, all he tried to do was to reach the next level in the game:

> 'I never set out to be captain. All I wanted to do was to play at the next level, because that was what my dad would want. If I was playing with the Under-11s the next thing for him was playing for the Under-12s or Under-15s, the Essex second team and so on. When I was chosen for the England team I couldn't believe I was there. Playing for England was all I wanted to do. That was enough for me.'

Heather Rabbatts, the former leader of Lambeth Council and now chair of Millwall Football Club, trained as a barrister but took the decision to move into local government. 'I love the law but you are always intervening at a moment of crisis in someone's life. I thought that if I could get involved with public policy, I could make a difference and that has always been a very important value to me and one that I have brought to whatever I have done.' Rabbatts was appointed as chief executive of the London Borough of Lambeth after responding to an advertisement for 'possibly the worst job in local government'. Years later, she accepted her role at Millwall Football Club because she recognized an organization that needed to change:

> 'Millwall had certain characteristics that I am drawn to. It was seen as irredeemable by some people. It was a "bad brand", as

Lambeth was, which needed to be redefined and reinvented. The aim with Lambeth initially was just to take it out of the headlines, to make it normal. And I didn't leave it with every problem sorted out but I felt it was no longer the "basket case" it was once considered to be.'

As well as the environment they were raised in, the leaders were also heavily influenced by a range of people, from parents to teachers and the people they worked for and with during their early career. In the next chapter we look at how the approach of future leaders can be influenced by existing leaders.

Chapter 3
Influences

Setting an example is not the main means of influencing others; it is the only means.

Albert Einstein

In the previous chapter we looked at how leaders can be shaped by their background, their family environment and the experiences of their early years. The people that future leaders meet along the way to their eventual role at the head of an organization also have the power to influence their future actions. Consciously or subconsciously, we learn from the people who surround us. We watch their actions and begin to understand what works in certain situations and what does not. Nasser Hussain is not alone in saying that almost everything that has influenced his career and his leadership style has been taken from someone he met along the way. 'You soak things up all the time, from what people can do but also from what they can't,' he explains.

Lord Inge argues that a small number of leaders are lucky enough to be born with natural ability and will rise to the top almost regardless of what goes on around them. Equally, some people will never become leaders. The rest, he says, lie somewhere in the middle and whether they eventually rise to a leadership position or not depends to a large extent on the people they meet and work for and with.

Our leaders cite a wide range of people that have influenced the way they themselves behave as leaders, from parents and teachers to colleagues, bosses and even people they have never met. Lord Inge, for example, says that everyone needs a hero and his is Field Marshal Slim, commander of the 14th Army in Burma during the Second World War and the author of *Defeat into Victory*:

'I was never going to be a regular soldier but I read that book and thought, this man is something very special. I joined the Royal Warwickshire Regiment because of that book. He had an influence on me even as a schoolboy.'

THE INFLUENCE OF PARENTS

Parents were a profound influence in the lives of many of our leaders, for a variety of reasons. Some – most notably the military leaders – had strong fathers and subsequently followed them in their chosen career. But even those with less obviously influential or charismatic parents say that they were an important influence on their future choices, behaviour and eventual leadership style.

Colonel Bob Stewart says that his father was 'the major motivator in my life' and as far as he was concerned, there was no other career for him but to follow his father into the military. It is not unusual that the greatest impact Colonel Stewart's father made on his son was in the way he talked to and treated the people reporting to him. It is an approach that Colonel Stewart himself employed throughout his own career.

'I watched how my father talked to his soldiers. His respect for his soldiers was absolute and complete. When he died, two of his drivers paid a lot of money to travel a long distance so they could say goodbye to him. That impressed me. I don't think that Sandhurst taught me leadership as much as my father. His style of leadership influenced me a great deal.'

Major General Patrick Cordingley also says that he was strongly influenced by his father's approach to leadership, and emulated his behaviour during his own career:

'My father and his friends in the Armed Forces always behaved in a way that seemed to be a comfortable way of getting on with people. They were very polite and thoroughly nice people that one tried to aspire to be like.'

In the case of leaders from the world of sport, it is often the case that their parents had a more direct impact on their behaviour during their childhood, usually because the parents were involved in their coaching to some extent. Sebastian Coe was coached by his father and says he 'never really questioned the level of work and commitment' that was required during his training. 'Probably, in fairness, most 14- or 15-year-olds would have balked at it,' he says. 'The important thing I learned from my father was that you have to know how to accept direction before you can give it. I also had it drummed into me from an early age that you were never going to win unless you had done all the hard work first. That was the passport.'

Coe also learned from the way his father managed the team that surrounded them during his athletics career:

'My father was a first-rate manager and was smart enough to know that he did not need to be the greatest expert on nutrition or biomechanics in the world. He brought people in as and when they were needed and formed a team around me. He set the strategy and direction on the extra levels of information we needed. I guess, in a way, that's what I've tried to do here [at the London Organising Committee for the Olympic and Paralympic Games].'

The former England rugby captain Martin Johnson was not coached by his parents but says that his mother, a national-level long distance runner, was a strong influence during his youth. He credits her with much of his fitness level and stamina:

> *'I used to go running in the hills with her when I was about 14 and she would have been in her mid-40s – you always think at that age that your life is the norm and it's only when you get out of it that you realize that it isn't. She ran sub-three hour marathons at that time as a veteran. She was tough at training. She never said, "You've done enough for now". She had no pace but could just go on forever. There was no self-pity at all. You worked hard, and that was good.'*

Even parents that appeared to outsiders to be quiet and low-key had, in some cases, a profound influence on our leaders. Greg Dyke says that his father was a cautious and quiet man and yet 'was a profound influence on us all, in all sorts of things that he said and did'. One particular quality of his father's that Dyke later emulated was his interest in people, irrespective of their position. 'He would talk to the roadsweeper and laugh at pomposity. He believed that everyone was worthy of respect. I was more likely at every place I've worked to like the people on reception more than I like the people on the board. You need the people who work in an organization to be on your side.'

Heather Rabbatts believes that she is a product of both parents, who had starkly contrasting personalities and backgrounds:

> *'My father was a quiet, introverted man whereas my mother was born in Jamaica, and was one of the first black models, a huge extrovert. So you couldn't have two bigger contrasts in character and personality. My father was enormously loyal; he never complained about anything and felt you should do your duty, whereas my mother was creative and difficult.*

'My dad gave me a sense of focus, structure and discipline, partly because he was in the army and partly because he was self-educated and came from a very poor family in Peckham. My mother felt isolated from her large Jamaican family when we moved to Kent in the late 1950s and never really adjusted. So she brought me up to believe that I should always be independent, get a good education and have my own money, but at the same time you should look after your family.

'My mum had great passion and creativity but if it all got a bit difficult, she would give up. My dad believed you should stick with it and shouldn't let people down. The single most important gift that my mother gave me was that you could do anything if you put your mind to it. It didn't matter whether my teacher said I was a failure, none of that mattered as long as you had a sense of self-belief.'

THE INFLUENCE OF TEACHERS

Teachers do not always get the recognition they deserve, but educators from primary school onwards can all take comfort from the fact that many of our leaders can claim that a teacher has had a major impact on their life. Sharkey Ward even remembers Mr Green, one of his teachers at primary school. 'I've never forgotten what a great guy he was. He encouraged me in everything, from academics to sport to country dancing.' Sue Campbell remembers the principal at her PE college, Eileen Alexander. 'She was a woman of substance, very principled, with great values. I still have contact with her and she's still a remarkable person, by anybody's standards. She had a big influence on me.'

For some, the influence of a teacher was to have a significant impact on the direction of their life. Martin Glenn, who attended a local comprehensive school after failing the 11-plus exam, says the support of an English teacher at his school was pivotal to his future career:

'I got a good set of O levels and went on to do A levels and was applying to university. I was convinced that I wanted to do something sensible and practical, so applied to do business studies and economics and things like that. Mr Parker asked me if I had thought of applying to Oxford or Cambridge. I hadn't, and had no idea how to go about it. I wouldn't have been able to navigate it by myself but he did it all for me. I think he was being a bit sly and had probably sensed that the Oxbridge colleges were being a bit sensitive about social inclusion, so we had a chance. So I did the entrance exam, had an interview and got accepted to Merton College Oxford to study politics, philosophy and economics.'

Gail Rebuck also says that she might not have considered university if her Spanish teacher had not suggested it:

'Nobody in my family had been to university and I genuinely didn't consider it. I thought you left school and went out to work. She explained the whole thing to me and, with her encouragement, I ended up applying.'

For Kevin Roberts, the influence of a teacher meant the difference between being written off at the age of 17 and a fulfilling and exciting career. Roberts was expelled from his grammar school when his girlfriend (soon to be his wife) became pregnant:

'It was the end of my world. I was going to stay at school, go to university and be successful. After I was expelled a man called Norman Ellis, who was deputy head of the comprehensive school in my home town, took me under his wing. He was also chairman of the local rugby club and cricket team and he made me captain of the rugby team at the age of 18 and put me in the first cricket XI before I was really ready. He gave me plenty of responsibility, nurtured me and counselled me. I'm still friends with him to this day.'

THE INFLUENCE OF BOSSES

People invariably soak up lessons from the bosses they have had during their career, whether by observing what works as a leader, or knowing what they responded to as a member of their team. Equally, people learn from poor leaders what behaviour to avoid. Martin Glenn argues that the employer-employee relationship is two-way and a good employee can shape his or her leader into something better.

Bosses, of course, have the power to influence a career directly and some of our leaders have been fortunate enough to work for people who have actively forwarded their career. Gail Rebuck recognizes that she has learned something from almost every boss she has had, and says she was extraordinarily lucky in that all of them supported and nurtured her. The first, the owner of a children's books packaging business, was sympathetic to her desire to learn about publishing and allowed her to attend a day release course at the London College of Printing. Her second boss was highly entrepreneurial and gave her a great deal of responsibility at an early stage. Her third was another entrepreneur and together they set up Century Publishing, and later, after the company was acquired by Random House, her US chief executive put her in charge of Random House in the UK when, she says, there were more obvious candidates for the job. 'He took a risk and I will be forever grateful,' she says.

Your first experience of a leader inevitably makes an impression, whether it is good or bad. In Dame Stella Rimington's case, her first job as a junior archivist with Worcester County Record Office put her in the path of a leader who was eccentric but effective:

> '*He had been a sergeant in the army and had one of those personalities that was moulded by the war. He ran the office almost like a branch of the military. If he wanted one of us he would tap out a Morse code signal on the bell system that was set up in the office and we would have to come running. Because he was my first boss, the first person I'd ever seen running anything, he did have an influence on me. He instilled a kind of culture on this disparate*

group of people. We were all fired by his massive enthusiasm. We all knew what he wanted us to do and that he would make jolly well sure we did it. But he also managed to create a kind of family feeling, which was quite strange because he always called us by our surnames. There was no informality, but we all felt we belonged to his family. So if you analyse it in terms of management it was a combination of setting a clear direction, while also making sure that we were personally involved in what was going on.'

Effective leadership comes in many different styles and some of our leaders have seen in practice that leaders who are very different in personality and approach can produce equally effective results. Martin Glenn says that he learned a great deal from two bosses he worked under while at Pepsico. Roger Enrico was chairman and CEO of the company from 1996, when Glenn was beginning to rise through the senior ranks of the organization, until 2001. In that year, Steve Reinemund took over as CEO and chairman until he stepped down in 2006. Glenn says that while the two men were remarkably different in personality and in leadership style, he responded well to the individual qualities displayed by both:

'Roger Enrico was just a brilliant guy – he was analytically very quick but he also had emotional intelligence. He was an extremely good reader of people and was intellectually curious. He was some- one you would aspire to be because he had touches of sheer class about him. He'd take people off to his ranch in Montana in groups of 12 and talk about leadership and so on. The warmth evoked by people who went on those courses is not something you forget.

'Steve Reinemund was very different. He's very hard, an ex-Marine, deeply religious, an awkward kind of guy socially. Enrico had a lot of presence but Steve didn't really have the command of an audi- ence. But when he talked about integrity he just absolutely had us. He did simplicity beautifully well. He'd treat people and issues on their merits, without bringing much baggage. He would confront awkward questions in a way that some people wouldn't. He had

the ability to ask those same simple questions. It was massively effective.'

The former England rugby captain Martin Johnson says that he has borrowed elements of his leadership style from two very different captains he played under during his earlier career. Dean Richards was captain of the Leicester side during Johnson's early career, while Will Carling captained the England team between 1993 and 1996. Whereas Richards had his roots in amateur rugby and worked part-time as a policeman during his playing career, Carling was a product of the professional era. Perhaps as a result, they were entirely different personalities. Richards was consciously and deliberately one of the team. 'He would just turn up and get on with the job. It was all about the way he was on the field. He was someone you wanted to have on your team.' Carling was more aloof from the players, says Johnson, and thought carefully about what made the players tick. 'I remember one game in Paris in 1994 when we had a lot of young guys on the team and were feeling quite nervous because we had lost the previous home game. Will came back to the dressing room after taking the toss and said he had seen the French team and they were all looking incredibly tense. At that moment, that was just what we needed to hear. I nicked the idea myself and used it before the Lions played South Africa in 1997.'

Nasser Hussain says he also learned a lot from the captains he played with during his cricketing career, many of whom had contrasting styles. He names Graham Gooch and Keith Fletcher as particularly influential, Fletcher because of his man management and tactical ability, and Gooch because of his professional attitude and dedicated preparation before each game. Mike Atherton, he says, led by example. 'When a man goes out at Johannesburg and bats for two and a half days and makes 180 in order to save a game, he's showing his team that you don't just roll over and die. I learned from a lot of captains.'

For Heather Rabbatts, her chief executive while working at Hammersmith and Fulham local authority, Tony Eddison, was influential in showing her a different style of leadership than she had encountered previously:

> '*He had a notice on his door that said, "Please feel free to pop in at any time". That sent a real shockwave through an organization where the previous chief executive was not like that at all. I learnt a huge amount in terms of how he brought his own emotional intelligence to the role, in terms of working with people. That was the first time I had seen a man lead in a different way.*'

She adds that her involvement with other organizations in an advisory role also helped to show her how effective bosses work in practice. While a governor at the BBC she was involved with the decision to recruit Greg Dyke as director general:

'Greg has enormous presence and charisma and what was interesting about that was that I knew when we interviewed him what we wanted him to do with the role. The BBC needed to be re-energized creatively and Greg did that. He is a man who can talk to a huge range of people and he took on what seemed like a pretty impossible job. I learned a great deal from observation.'

Bosses also have the potential to influence behaviour in a more general way. Sebastian Coe says that while he was an MP, he learned from watching his friend and the then Conservative Party Leader, William Hague. The lessons he learned, though, were not about particular leadership but about a risk-taking attitude

> '*I liked the fact that in a funny sort of way he took on a position which probably didn't give him the best chance of developing his career. He was smart enough to know that taking leadership of a party when it had been in opposition for so long and there were plenty of rumblings was a risky business. But he was prepared to take the risk on the simple basis that some doors don't open twice. You have to take a chance.*'

'It's a bit like going into a race, I guess. So many athletes go into a race with a plan to run the first 200m in so many seconds and then ease off in the back straight. But the reality is that there are nine other people on the track with their own gameplan, so you have to be flexible – but not flexible to the point that you are compromising.'

Even if there is no particularly influential leader in an organization, a working environment can still have the power to shape and influence a future leader. Sir Clive Woodward remembers one of his first jobs, working for Xerox as a management trainee:

'The training I got at Xerox was excellent, but it was a very aggressive world, it was all about league tables. You had to be totally single minded. You sank or swam. You got a pat on the back or you got shot, and that's not so different from professional sport.'

Perhaps because of the structured hierarchy in which they operate, our military leaders can all recall more than one officer or commander that had a profound impact on the way they would later operate as a leader. Colonel Bob Stewart recalls an instructor at Sandhurst who impressed him because of a leadership style that was in stark contract to many others that he had encountered. 'There were all sorts of Sergeant Majors who made us stomp around and so on but he was always gently spoken and talked decently to us. He said things like how we should never run because it panics the men, or raise our voice. To me, he was an ideal model.'

Major General Patrick Cordingley says that he and other young officers were always very conscious of watching how officers in slightly higher ranks operated. 'You might see a General covered in medal ribbons and that could be very impressive but you could not know what made him tick, whereas we knew what made our commanding officer tick. And if they were fine men, that had an effect on the way you behaved yourself.' The officers Major General Cordingley met during his early career undoubtedly influenced his own leadership style:

'I liked people who were reasonable, people who spent time getting to know you and who led by example rather than by authority. We used to go on lengthy exercises in Germany and we would watch officers under pressure, seeing how they reacted and whether they got bad-tempered when they were tired. The people I respected were the ones that didn't let sleep deprivation cloud the issue. They were the people who affected me and that was what I wanted to aspire to. There were some extraordinarily fine examples in the other ranks who had the authority and stripes but managed to get the soldiers to do what they wanted to do by using their personality and being encouraging to them.'

Sharkey Ward says that JJ Black, captain of HMS Invincible, in which Sharkey's Sea Harrier squadron was stationed during the Falklands conflict, was a significant influence for similar reasons. 'He was a wonderful, brilliant guy. He had a sense of humour and compassion that kept everyone happy throughout the war and he spoke to everyone on the same level.' Earlier in his career, he remembers being profoundly impressed with Admiral Sir David Luce, who was First Sea Lord between 1963 and 1966:

'He used to do amazing things to communicate with his men and try and find out what they were thinking. For instance he would put on a Navy ratings uniform and go down to the dockside incognito and help the men who were loading supplies onto the ships, carrying things up the gangways with them, just so he could get to know them and what they were all about. He was amazing – loved by everyone. That proved to me that no-one should be on a pedestal as leader. They should know the people who work for them and know them well. That stuck with me.'

All of the military leaders can remember clear events where important lessons were learned, sometimes from unlikely sources. Lord Inge tells of an early conversation he had with his Regimental Sergeant Major when he was a young Second Lieutenant:

'I had gone into the Sergeant's Mess to collect the takings and Regimental Sergeant Major Calvert was waiting for me there, in uniform. He invited me to sit at his table. Then he said that he had seen me earlier at the barracks and had seen a soldier who failed to salute me, and that it was clear that I had known that he didn't salute me and had done nothing about it. He said that personally he didn't care whether the British Army required its soldiers to salute an officer or not, but said that if I did not have the courage – and he meant the moral courage – to correct him in barracks, I may not have the moral courage to correct him on far more important matters when we were on operations and there was a risk that he could be wounded or lose his life as a result. "Private Johnson," he said, "will be outside Support Company later and although you can't charge him for it now, you will make it quite clear to him that it won't happen again. The Company Sergeant Major will be in the background if you need any help." That was an important lesson for me and the fact that he took the trouble to talk to me, an indifferent second lieutenant, about it was wonderful. Although I didn't think so at the time.'

MENTORS AND MENTORING

In spite of the influences of teachers, parents, bosses and others throughout their lives, our leaders have mixed views towards the concept of mentoring. Lord Inge says that while he has worked for some remarkable people during his career he has a dislike of structured mentoring systems because the most important element, a rapport between the mentor and mentoree, is impossible to predict or plan.

Many of our leaders admitted that the leadership role can be a lonely one and some, such as Sue Campbell, felt that they would have benefited from a mentor during their career. Some formed friendships that could be described as a mentoring relationship, although they were never formalized. Dame Stella Rimington, for example, says she would often talk through issues and problems with a colleague at MI5 who was on a similar level in the organization but was not in competition for the senior role. 'I wouldn't say it was a formal mentoring relationship but it was very useful because he felt completely free to tell me what he thought and I valued his opinion, particularly because I knew it was disinterested. We were very different so I would not always follow his advice, but it was very valuable having someone who was able to tell me things from a point of view different from my own.'

Kevin Roberts freely admits that he would have struggled to achieve as much in his career had it not been for a range of mentors.

> 'The mentor role has been a great influence on me, in both work and life. I'm at my best when I'm coached, guided and mentored. I'm not at my best when I have a boss who tells me what to do. I'm not at my best if I don't have someone helping me out. To this very day I have a mentor on all things about me and all things about business, someone I have been friends with for 10 or 12 years. It isn't any new age executive coaching crap, it's people who have looked out for me and now I spend a lot of my time looking out for them. You learn as much from looking out for mentors as you do from mentors looking out for you.'

The leaders we spoke to have subsequently applied many of the lessons they learned from the people who influenced them during their development and early working lives throughout the later stages of their career. In the next chapters we will look at the major demands placed on leaders in all fields, from developing, communicating and implementing direction within the organization to encouraging the best possible performance from the people who work for them.

PART TWO

Chapter 4
Vision

The very essence of leadership is that you have to have a vision. You can't blow an uncertain trumpet.

Theodore Hesburgh

If people are going to follow a leader, it helps if everyone involved understands very clearly where they are heading. No leader can afford to be vague about the purpose of the organization and their plans for the future, both immediate and long-term, as Sue Campbell of UK Sport explains:

'I learnt by trial and error that good leadership means you have a very clear vision about where you're going and a clear sense of purpose. If people are going to join you, they need to know what

mission you are on – your values and passion. It's not simply a job.
I want to make a difference in sport. I want to make a difference in
a world that I really understand and which has made a difference
for me.'

In this chapter we will look at how our leaders form and communicate the vision for their organization. According to John Kotter, the direction-setting aspect of leadership creates visions or strategies that 'describe a business, technology or corporate culture in terms of what it should become over the long term, and articulate a feasible way of achieving this goal'.[1] He adds that the process is not mystical but a 'tough, sometimes exhausting process of gathering and analysing information. People who articulate such visions are not magicians but broad-based thinkers who are willing to take risks'.

In Kotter's view, a vision or strategy does not have to be brilliantly innovative and indeed, he says that some of the best are not. A good vision, he says, serves three important purposes:

- It clarifies the general direction of the organization, simplifying hundreds or thousands of more detailed decisions;
- It motivates people to take action in the right direction; and
- It helps coordinate the actions of a wide collection of individuals.

What is crucial is not the originality of the vision, Kotter argues, but how well it serves the interest of constituents and how easily it can be translated into a realistic competitive strategy.

We should add that our leaders are split over the term 'vision' and do have contrasting views of what they mean when they talk about the agenda or plan for their organization's future. Lord Inge, for instance, says he dislikes the concept of vision statements and prefers to talk in terms of creating an overall 'ethos' for an organization, based on a deep understanding of what makes it tick. Kevin Roberts of Saatchi & Saatchi also bridles at the term:

'The role of a leader is to share a dream, not a vision statement. Martin Luther King did not stand up and say, "I have a vision statement". We all want to work for something bigger than a pay cheque and more important than producing the next laundry detergent. [Leaders] have to share a dream and then, within that, you have to steer and sustain the dream constantly because the reality is that people have a short attention span.'

CREATING THE VISION

Warren Bennis argues that all great organizations are built around a shared dream or motivating purpose. The reality, though, is that many mission statements can be vague, meaningless or buried in management-speak. The accepted view is that the vision should be simple, inspiring, focused, but realistic. 'Your team need not believe that it is literally saving the world,' says Bennis. 'It is enough to feel it is helping people in need or battling a tough competitor. Simply punching a time clock doesn't do it.'[2]

Many leaders inherit a mission (or vision) from their predecessors and subsequently adapt it. Others feel that they simply identified and articulated a vision that was already present, but not recognized. It is comparatively rare for a leader to form an entirely new vision for their organization. One of the few that has done so is Charles Dunstone, chief executive of Carphone Warehouse, who set up the company with David Ross in the late 1980s. He explains that the idea for a business grew out of a visionary concept:

'I am a bit of an idealist and my original idea was to create a successful business that respected its customers and treated its employees with dignity. In other words, to have a successful business and still care for people. I felt that the high street rivals to our business were absolutely failing to do that. One of the sad things about getting older and doing things for longer is that there is a danger that you become too rational. You accept compromise. That's why all politicians should be in their 20s. Trying to achieve the impossible is what makes organizations great.'

A number of the leaders we spoke to argue that a clear vision has been vital to the success of their organization. Sebastian Coe became chairman of the board of the London 2012 Olympic Games and Paralympic Games Bid Committee in May 2004, just over a year before the final decision was due to be made on the winning bid by the International Olympics Committee. The mission of the organization was not in doubt: to win the bid. What was less clear was *why* its mission was to win the bid.

In the case of the Bid Committee, the vision was relatively unusual in that it would have a wide application – and required widespread appeal – outside the organization. In other words, it should be an unselfish vision with ethical appeal that alluded to a higher purpose than some of the inward-looking and self-centred visions adopted by many commercial organizations.

Coe felt that in order for the London bid to be successful, there had to be a clear vision that was inspirational, could be clearly articulated and that was as unique as possible. The vision would also have to be carried forward to a fast-growing organization, should the bid be successful. Coe explains how and his team created a formal vision for the Committee:

'When I joined the Bid Committee we had a collection of hugely talented people but I did sense that the transport people just wanted to build the best transport system in the world and the security people just wanted to create the best security system in the world. No-one was really answering the question, "Why?"

'We had rather buried ourselves in the technical side of things, which was important because you do need to be a predominately good bid technically in order to persuade the International Committee. But we needed to go back to basics a little and sit down and think about why we were doing this. It wasn't to build a better railway. It wasn't to build the best and most inventive stadium. It wasn't to boost tourist numbers. It wasn't to show the world that we have better shopping in Knightsbridge than you have along the Champs Elysées. It was to get more bloody kids into sport.

'I don't get excited at the thought of moving 25,000 people in and out of a tunnel every hour, I get excited about moving 25,000 people through a tunnel because I want these Games to have the best possible atmosphere. I want as many young people there as possible, on reasonable ticket prices, so they can experience something that might regain some of the excitement of sport for them.'

This personal view, says Coe, had grown following two conversations he had had with his children. Three years before, his daughter had commented that none of the children in her class was aware that the World Athletics Championship was underway in Paris, when she had visited the games with her father. And about six months later, his two sons had been 'absolutely speechless' to hear that their father could not name the world's most famous skateboarder. 'Those two events were like a signpost exploding out of the ground for me,' says Coe. 'I was very close to this marketplace and yet I had not fully recognized that the sport that I had been involved in for most of my life was drifting off people's radar screens.'

With these ideas at the back of his mind, Coe says that he sat down everyone in his team in a room for two days, with the help of external facilitators to make sure that the group did not talk themselves around in circles, in order to create a vision for the organization and for the London Games as a whole. 'I always knew that we were going to be about engaging the next generation, about taking the chance to regenerate a large part of East London and about getting sport higher up the political and social agenda,' he says. Those ideas were 'drilled and drilled and drilled' over two days until the team came up with the simplest possible vision: 'It was to inspire young people. That was why we were here.' (The official vision statement of the London Organising Committee for the Olympic Games and Paralympic Games, which was set up after the bid was successful and of which Coe is now chair, is 'to stage inspirational games that capture the imagination of young people around the world and leave a lasting legacy'.) The formation of that vision, he says, was vital to the success of the Olympic bid:

'It was remarkable that once we understood that and had bought into it, it became so much more. When you are talking about a campaign you tend to have 10 balls in the air at once. As my father used to say, it's important not to play with too many variables at once and just focus on the core things that you need to do.'

Sue Campbell makes a similar point about her organization, UK Sport, which, she says, lacked a clear central vision when she was appointed as Reform Chair of the organization in 2003 (she was appointed chair in 2005). The agency was set up by Royal Charter in 1996 with the aim of 'working in partnership to lead sport in the UK to world class success':

'We work in a complex sporting landscape so we need to be clear about what we stand for, what we care about and what we're best at. When I joined we had a large range of objectives. Now we have three and they are very simple. We are about winning more medals for the UK. We're about having world-class standards in terms of drugs education and testing in sport. And we're about having influence on the world stage. Those are our three areas and our job is to be world class in the way we deliver each of them.'

A clear vision for the future can also serve to motivate a team that may have become jaded about its objectives. Martin Glenn tells of his encounter with the marketing director at Mars relatively early on in his career:

'I was brought into the company as cat food marketing manager and on the first day the marketing director asked me what share of the cat food market we had as a company. I said we had a 43.3% share. He said no, what we had was a 43.3% share of the prepared cat food market. There were five million cats in the country and prepared food only accounted for 60% of their daily calories. The rest of the time they were eating scraps and other stuff. So we looked at the things we were not providing, and milk was one of them. Why not produce milk especially for cats? So we came out

with a premium price lactose-free milk, which made Mars a lot of money. The point is, you sometimes need to see the wider picture. He had the idea and led me to it. As a marketing specialist, it was massively motivating.'

Glenn is now chief executive of Birds Eye Iglo, which was formed when Unilever sold off its frozen foods business to a private-equity funded buyer, and creating a new vision for the organization was one of his first tasks in the role. The company was described at the time as the largest frozen foods business in Europe, but Glenn emphasizes the importance of articulating a vision – or story, as he calls it – for the company that was more likely to motivate its employees. In Glenn's case he took the view that Warren Bennis has often spoken of, that a real (or invented) enemy can be a strong motivational factor for an organization and its people:

'What benefit have any of us gained from Birds Eye being the biggest in Europe? All it meant is that we were the biggest and the fastest declining. We needed an enemy dead fast. Our enemy is chilled food – frozen food is a much smaller market than chilled food and a much less important one. It's much more fun being an underdog in a turnaround situation than it is being the big beast. It appealed to people's basic human emotions about where they'd rather be.'

Greg Dyke also changed the BBC's official vision statement as part of the 'Making It Happen' culture change programme he oversaw while director general of the organization. The vision of the previous director-general, John Birt had been 'to be the best-managed public sector organization in the world'. As part of the culture change programme, Dyke announced to staff that the new vision for the organization was 'to become the most creative organization in the world'. While Birt's vision was worthy and laudable, says Dyke, it was not particularly well suited to a creative organization such as the BBC: 'The best-run public sector organization in the world? No-one gets out of bed for that.'

Gail Rebuck, who took over as chief executive of Random House UK in 1991, says that while she felt a clear vision was important for the organization, she was concerned that a classic business vision statement would be rejected because of the creative environment Random operated in. 'I was appointed in fairly dramatic circumstances when my previous boss was fired so I had to get my head around the challenge fairly quickly. My first thought was that I needed to say something that would define what I believed in. Not a vision statement exactly, but an internal statement for the company. I said that what we had to do was balance creativity with profitability. If you're not creative then you will never take the risks that will lead to profit and if you're not profitable then you won't have the money to take creative risks in the first place. I think that resonated with people.'

Rebuck says she initially resisted forming an official vision statement for the company. 'Publishers are very creative people who tend to be allergic to management speak,' she explains. 'I was concerned that I'd have them running for the hills.' Eventually, though, when the company was more stable, she felt it was important to clearly articulate what it stood for:

'We did it quite scientifically as a board and tried to articulate why people came to work motivated every day and excited about the job to be done. We decided that we were about cultural diversity and we existed to publish books that enrich everyone's lives. I hope this resonated with all staff, whatever their function. We then formed a whole series of statements around innovation, discovering new writers, about protecting our heritage and our commitment to literacy. Basically it was all about the things we were already doing but which had not been properly articulated before.'

COMMUNICATING THE VISION

Forming a vision is only half of the battle. 'It's not just about writing a mission statement or producing a vision,' says Brian Morgan of Cardiff Business School, 'it needs to be much more passionate than that. It requires aligning the core values and purpose of the business with everything the company does – including decision-making, recruitment, staff development, product development and customer care. Crafting a mission and creating a vision and embedding them into the business are necessary ingredients of successful companies. It takes time and it also requires commitment and passion to make it work.'

The process of communicating the overall vision or strategy throughout the organization is vital to its success. John Kotter characterizes this process as 'aligning people', or 'communicating the new direction to those who can create coalitions that understand the vision and are committed to its achievement'.[3] As Kotter says, the target audience for this will probably encompass many people outside of the organization, such as suppliers, shareholders and even customers.

In his book *Leading Change*, Kotter argues that undercommunication of an organization's vision is one of the primary reasons why transformational initiatives often fail. Kotter identifies three common and recurring patterns of ineffective communication:[4]

- A good vision is developed but only a small fraction of the intra-company communication is used to sell it, with the result that most people in the organization remain unaware that it exists;
- A vision is developed and the leader spends a great deal of time communicating it to managers, who subsequently fail to cascade the message down through the organization; or
- A vision is developed and a great deal of time and effort is put into communicating it throughout the organization, but the effort is undermined when some key, highly visible individuals behave in ways that are antithetical to the vision, resulting in widespread cynicism among employees.

The leaders we spoke to agree on a number of key points that Kotter also observed as vital elements in the successful communication of vision throughout an organization. In general, the leaders agree that in order to get the message across successfully, it has to be easy to understand, consistent, and repeated as often as is necessary. The leaders also make frequent use of analogy and metaphor as a way of communicating the message in an accessible way.

One of the first challenges for a leader will be to express the vision in terms that are understandable and of appeal to the target audience. John Kotter makes the point that well-chosen words can make a message memorable, particularly when coupled with the use of powerful imagery. Martin Glenn would agree with this, saying that 'any leader of a large people organization needs to have something of the politician and the marketer about them'. Glenn feels it is important to keep expressing where you want the organization to go in terms of the benefits that will be gathered and says that there are particular buttons that a leader can push, depending on the demographics of the work force. 'These days, especially for anyone under the age of 30, if you're not appealing to their sense of civic responsibility and their wish to protect the environment, you're not going to enlist them in any change programme whatsoever. You have to understand the role of your employees as citizens and parents and so on. It's about pitching the objective in quasi-political terms that appeals to all sorts of parts of an individual's make-up.'

Glenn believes that the most effective way of getting the message across, particularly in a large organization, is by structuring a clear narrative of where the business is at the moment, and where it wants to be. 'People respond well to stories. We remember emotions better than we do fact,' he says. 'They can't remember the day that Neil Armstrong walked on the moon, but they can remember where they were.'

When Glenn was appointed chief executive of the Walkers business, he says, the organization was seriously underperforming:

'This was a story where we had to go on attack, and attack our competitors. If we could grow market share, good things would happen. So we focused on market share. I did that very hokey thing of saying that we had a market share of 40%, and it needed to be 60%. We even called it Project 60. It wasn't a particularly clever narrative idea, but it worked better than it should have done. The

point was that there was a mini crisis which needed a number and a time frame, so people understood it.'

Sue Campbell of UK Sport often uses the same technique. 'If I am trying to express the power of sport to someone whose only view of sport is that it is football, I'll tell them how sport changed Jack's life at school. If I haven't got them captivated by the end then I haven't succeeded. It is stories that help you express what really matters, the real power of sport to change lives. Real life stories about individuals are far more moving than theoretical models.'

Gail Rebuck also sees the benefits of formulating a vision or strategy in terms of a story. 'When I talk to my board I say that every year we have to develop a new story. What is the purpose of this year? Where are we going? It can be a development of the previous year's story but there always has to be a story. Sometimes we can dictate it and sometimes it is dictated to us, like when a rival buys another publisher and becomes larger than we are. We have to rewrite our storybook because we're no longer number one. When that actually happened, after 10 years at number 1, I said, what fun, we've got something to strive for.'

Even with the aid of a story, getting the message across is often as simple as repeating the message over and over until it is heard. Gail Rebuck says she communicated her vision for Random House through 'three or four years of constant repetition'. Even so, she was initially hesitant about introducing the concept of a vision statement for the company to its employees:

'I was very careful about the way I introduced it. I didn't want to just stand up one day at a sales conference and say, "Hey guys, here's our vision statement". So I was conversational about it. I said that sometimes we had to wonder to ourselves why we came to work. It wasn't just about making money, although it was understood that we had to make money. We come to work because we all believe in book publishing and care about it and in a small way, through our books, we change people's lives. The question was how we articulated that. No-one heard it at first but after a while

[the vision] became very ingrained in the company. It becomes real, part of the company's DNA.'

For Sebastian Coe, communicating the vision for his organization had far wider implications since it was fundamental to the success of the bid to win the Olympic and Paralympic Games. Coe knew that the chances of the Committee winning the bid depended heavily on the people within the Bid Committee buying into the vision, and then communicating it effectively to outsiders. His gut instinct in May 2004, 14 months before the end of the bidding process, was that few people believed that London could win the Games:

> *'Most people felt that we couldn't win for reasons of transport or a lack of public backing or government support and I was conscious that if that perception had not changed by the Olympic Games in August 2004 then the market would just move on and the chance would be lost. The market has an unnerving ability just to suddenly say collectively this was not going to happen and I knew that once we had gone past that point it would be very, very difficult to drag it back.*

> *'My priority was to get everybody thinking that the bid was winnable, in spite of what they had heard, in spite of what they had read and in spite of what they were being told in the local pub. We knew better than most why we were going for the bid and my gut feeling was that once we had articulated that we would have a much better chance of being able to communicate that externally. And that was the case.'*

The speech delivered by Coe to the voting committee in Singapore, which used this vision as a central theme, is credited as playing a critical part in London's successful bid. Coe says that, although the vision had been largely finalized in his mind a year before the Singapore meeting, he did not begin to articulate it in the form of the speech until two or three months before the meeting, when the films that would accompany the speech were commissioned. Coe then quietly road-tested the central idea with a carefully selected group of interested people from a variety of backgrounds, including a small number of IOC members. By the time it came to finalize the speech he would deliver at Singapore, the vision was as solid, well-developed and thoroughly tested as possible: 'The speech itself I wrote between four-thirty and six-thirty in the morning, two days after we arrived in Singapore, when I had jetlag.'

LONG OR SHORT TERM?

Once a vision is in place, the challenge for leaders is to steer the organization in that direction. This effectively means a careful balancing of the short-term and long-term view, keeping sight of the long-term mission while making sure that each step along the way will eventually take the organization closer to it. Heather Rabbatts describes this as 'taking the helicopter view', which allows her to maintain the clarity of the overall roadmap.

Martin Glenn believes that balancing the short and long term, as well as internal and external issues, is one of the most essential roles for a leader. He argues that companies can get swept up in the competitive nature of day-to-day life and as a result fail to concentrate sufficiently on the future of the business. Organizations, leaders and managers, he says, are faced every day with important and non-important tasks and with urgent and non-urgent tasks. The urgent, non-important tasks are a way of modern life and can sap an organization's energy. If it spends too long dealing with urgent, non-important tasks, the important, non-urgent tasks will be neglected, to the long-term detriment of the company. Glenn explains how he illustrates the balance between the short and long term within his own organization:

'I talk about it within my company in terms of having a healthy lifestyle. I try to do cardio exercises three times a week. I know how many units of alcohol I should be drinking and I know that I need to include a certain proportion of fruit and vegetables in my diet. If I don't do all that, nothing bad will happen in the next few weeks

but over time I know I'll put on weight and will be less healthy. The same thing applies with balancing the operations of today with the management of tomorrow. There's no immediate bad payoff if you don't get the knottier things done, but over time …'

Dame Stella Rimington, the former director-general of MI5, takes the view that as long as the overall vision is right, that should free the leader from too much involvement in short-term issues. 'As a leader I think you have to do far more looking to the future than you do dealing with the now,' she says. 'It seems to me that the actual detail of dealing with the now is not your business. Once you've set the culture and you have the right people around you and have communicated clearly what the three or four main issues are, then frankly you have to just let them get on with it.'

For other organizations, though, the only way to achieve a long-term objective is to concentrate on short-term strategy. Sir Clive Woodward's vision for the England rugby team was for them to be the best in the world, and that meant winning the World Cup. He explains, though, that achieving that vision was not about setting their sights on the final goal but on taking a series of small steps that could eventually lead them there:

'Our strategy to win the World Cup was to win the next game. A plan to win the World Cup in four years' time is just nonsense. We coached the team for next Saturday's game. Win that and the World Cup will take care of itself.'

Many of our leaders add that one of the challenges in communicating an overall vision to an organization lies in keeping people focused on the priorities. Martin Glenn says that the key is 'not to have too many priorities, and keep talking about them. It's that simple.' Dame Stella Rimington agrees. 'Ultimately,' she says, 'it comes down to trying to make sure that you don't have anything in your intray that you don't need. Once you do that and show quite clearly that there are three or four things you are focused on, further down the organization the same thing happens. Your employees are out there selling jumpers or stopping terrorists or whatever their role is, and what you are doing is putting everything in place that they need in order to be able to do that effectively.'

Sue Campbell says that she keeps an organization focused by actively showing that she is aware of everything that is going on:

'I make sure I read every weekly report and summary and listen to my colleagues. And then I make sure that if a member of staff has done well with something, I mention it and congratulate them. It's important that they know you know what's going on, and that you will know if they are not on task. I'm not being a school ma'am, they just need to be aware that you know, otherwise you become detached from the organization.'

In Chapter 11 we look more closely about communication in general, and in particular, at how leaders ensure that the overall vision is heard and understood throughout the organization.

WHAT LEADERS REALLY DO:
- Create a vision that:
  - is simple and accessible;
  - can be clearly articulated and easily understood;
  - can realistically be achieved; and
  - is designed to inspire employees.
- Use stories to appeal to basic human emotions in articulating the vision
- Create an artificial 'enemy' if necessary
- Repeat the message until it is understood
- Balance short term and long term priorities, but keep the long term objectives always in view.

---

[1] *What Leaders Really Do*, p87
[2] *The Secrets of Great Groups*
[3] *What Leaders Really Dol*, p86
[4] *Leading Change*, p 9

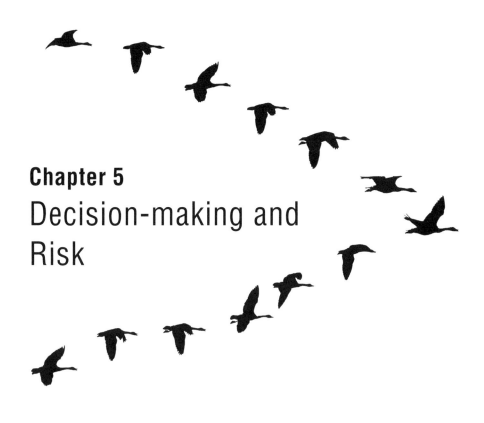

Chapter 5
Decision-making and Risk

You miss 100% of the shots you don't take.

Wayne Gretzky, Canadian ice hockey player

The job of any leader, in any walk of life, is to make decisions and then make sure that they are carried out. If the leader is fortunate, his or her followers will agree with and welcome the decision, and do their utmost to implement them on the leader's behalf. Any leader, though, will inevitably face a situation more than once where a decision is unwelcome and unsupported and has to be forced through.

In this chapter we will look at how leaders in a range of organizations approach decision-making. Later, we will look at how these leaders assess risk and take difficult decisions, and the lessons they have learned along the way.

When asked about how they approach the decision-making process, it was clear that all of our leaders had already carefully analysed their own personal style and methods. Martin Glenn says that his decision-making skills were learned at Oxford, where he completed a degree in politics, philosophy and economics:

'The course itself was inspiring and in particular I found the philosophy element fantastic conditioning in terms of being able to think clearly. I think it is what I have applied the most in my business career. It was just pure, hard thinking. A couple of hours a week spent in front of a man with three brains who just asked you to explain yourself a bit further was extremely good training. As a result of that course, I've always been pretty good at analytical thinking and simplifying complex problems. It has opened doors for me, going to Oxford.'

Glenn stresses, though, that decision-making in business is not necessarily about being right or wrong. 'As opposed to pure science, in commerce there are not that many objective right and wrongs. Being excellent in business is about being 80% right, especially when you are dealing with human behaviour and marketing. You can get direction and benchmarks about what works elsewhere, but you can never know for sure.' That said, Glenn adds that no leader can afford to be vague and they need to be able to recognize the root of an issue, even when swamped with information. 'One of the chief executives I have worked for used to say that a point of view is worth 1000 IQ points. A leader has to be able to weigh up the facts very quickly. Saying "This is the core of the problem" is far more useful than saying "I think we need another review".'

Some leaders are willing to admit that sometimes the best decision is not to make a decision at that time. Sue Campbell of UK Sport says she is an intuitive decision-maker rather than an instinctive one. 'If I don't know what the answer is, I will leave it and think about it. I'll often leave it a while to vegetate and then suddenly the answer will come to me, even though I might not have been thinking about it at the time.'

Dame Stella Rimington, who has undoubtedly had to make some of the most difficult judgements of all our leaders during her career as director general of MI5, says that she never agonized over them:

'What you have to do is to decide the right moment at which to take a decision. Very often people are pushing you to take a decision before you really need to, so the first question to ask is always, do we have to decide this now? And honestly, very often you don't and it is far better that you delay because you will often end up with more information that will help you make a better decision. But if you have no choice and have to decide there and then, you have to accept that you don't know everything but are doing what seems the right thing and if it turns out to be wrong well, too bad. No-one else could have done any better.'

Dame Stella adds that she was comfortable in admitting that she might not know the answer to a particular problem and in discussing options with her colleagues. She says she encouraged a collegiate form of leadership at MI5 and would seek as much input as possible before making a decision: 'You have to be very comfortable with your colleagues, though, to be able to do that. You also have to be reasonably self-confident because you are, in a sense, exposing your vulnerability and saying that you don't actually know the answer and need other people to help you.'

This was not a trait that was common to many of our leaders but was certainly more prevalent among the female leaders than the male. Heather Rabbatts argues that in general terms, the male leadership style tends towards the autocratic, whereas women are better at building consensus, although there are inevitably many exceptions, 'Margaret Thatcher being a great case in point'. Dame Stella Rimington agrees:

'I think that women do tend to be more collegiate. Women, on the whole, are less inclined to think that it's important to come to an instant conclusion or for the leader to demonstrate that he knows the answer to everything. I have seen male leaders, particularly

in the commercial world, who somehow magically immediately know the answer to the most complicated issue. Of course that doesn't inspire confidence because everybody else knows that he can't know the answer. There could be many answers and it's something that you've got to discuss. I think women find that easier, personally, though probably not all women.'

Even so, many of our male leaders are happy to admit that they do not always have the answers. Ron Dennis, chief executive of McLaren, says that 'no doubt one of the frustrations that people have when working with me is that I would rather not take a decision than make the wrong one'. The worst thing, in his view, that a leader can do in making a decision is to be emotional. 'That's why I have a reputation among many people for not smiling or showing emotion, but I think that's pretty easy to understand.' Dennis says that the key to his decision-making is thought, although in his field of work he does not always have the luxury of time:

'Thought is always the key to getting it right. But sometimes you have to make a spontaneous decision. You can't suddenly freeze-frame a Grand Prix. You have to take a decision that is based on intuition, experience, risk analysis, all of the things that leadership – especially in the military sense – finds itself forced to do. High risk is often linked to short-term decisions. That's why I rarely gamble. If I do gamble, it teaches me that you can only shorten the odds by being phenomenally competent and totally focused on the game.'

Leaders who work in creative organizations or consumer-led industries have specific difficulties that affect their ability to make effective decisions. Many agree that their position at the head of an organization puts them at risk of losing touch with the factors that enable them to make good decisions. Kevin Roberts, worldwide CEO of Saatchi & Saatchi, says that one of the things he believes about leadership is that 'the further up the company you go, the more stupid you become' because 'you are so far away from consumers, it's not funny'. He argues that it is increasingly difficult for a leader in a consumer-led organization to get valuable information because there is a risk that the people immediately around them either do not know it, or are unwilling to relay it to the leader. For that reason, at Saatchi & Saatchi he drives decision-making down the organization so it is as close to the consumer as possible:

'I'm aware that I'm stupid so I go out of my way to listen, to check and to ask. I also go out of my way to make sure that people don't do what I tell them and so I don't let them ask me for approval, I'm only willing to be consulted for advice, then it's back to them. My decision-making is limited to stuff that doesn't matter. We pass all our decision-making down to the people who have to make it work. In my view, it's better for a 25-year-old kid to be responsible for the decision because he'll work 24 hours on it. I could only give it 10 minutes. All you do is give the kid the resources and the nurturing and mentoring he needs and then get the hell out of his way. What's he going to do? How many things can wreck my business? Not many. As a leader you might make 80 decisions a day and 75 of them don't count, so stop making them.'

Martin Glenn agrees that decisions in a consumer-led business present specific problems. 'I've learned the hard way that observing the behaviour of people rather than listening to what they say is a much more powerful tool in making decisions,' he says. 'People treat market research as an intelligence test – they want to give you the right answer. Looking at behavioural benchmarks is underdone in business, I think. People move way too quickly to focus groups in Egham.' Glenn illustrates his point with two examples from his time as head of Walkers foods:

'When we launched Doritos [tortilla chips] in the UK in 1994, it had been tried three or four times before but the decision was based on our belief that this kind of product already worked in a market – they were very popular in the US – and we just had to find a way of presenting Doritos to the Brits in a way that went with the grain rather than against it. It was a product that had a track record else-

where so the mountains of market research that said people did or didn't like it needed to be given a sense of wider perspective.

'That said, rarely have I gone with gut feeling without there being some kind of evidence and analysis behind it. Lime flavoured tortilla chips was one example. The market research was horrible but we launched it because I liked them and my factory manager, who was a completely different character from me, also liked them. And bags kept disappearing from the marketing department, so other people liked them as well. Conceptually, lime flavoured tortilla chips didn't sound right, but they worked.'

Kevin Roberts sums this up by saying that '80% of consumer decisions are made emotionally, not rationally'. By accepting this view in a wider context, he believes, creative organizations can find the key to competitive advantage:

'We all have the same information, the same knowledge and the same facts. We have MBAs. We have the internet. If we all apply rationality and logic we all get to the same place. How does that result in competitive advantage? It doesn't. Competitive advantage in every business comes from innovation, and innovation comes from the generation of ideas, which comes from a culture of creativity. With business decisions, people often assemble a great roll of bankers and lawyers and they come to exactly the same decision as everyone else. So for me the thing I most believe in is that you should make the big decisions with your heart and the little ones with your head. But on the other hand you couldn't run a life insurance company like that, that would be ridiculous.'

MILITARY MISSION ANALYSIS

The consequences of making a poor decision are far more serious in the armed forces than they are in any other field. For that reason, the military takes a careful and structured approach to decision-making, known as mission analysis. Each individual step in the mission is analysed along with potential and known constraints and risks. As Major General Patrick Cordingley puts it, 'Once you get the mission you start to dissect it. You make absolutely certain that you understand exactly what it means. Then you consult and challenge the assumptions you have made.'

Mission analysis involves analysing the task and mission that has been set, your own requirements, capabilities, constraints, restrictions, any outside influences, as well as the strengths, intentions and capabilities of the enemy (if there is one) and the timeline. The aim of mission analysis is to be sure that the mission is clearly understood, that any variables have been considered and accounted for as far as possible, and that the best course of action to meet all of the factors has been identified.

Colonel Bob Stewart, who led UK forces under the UN in Bosnia, explains how the process works in practice:

'I was in Berlin when I was told that there was a plan to send a British unit to Bosnia. I was briefed and was in the Balkans 48 hours later. I wrote the mission analysis overnight after the briefing and wrote that my mission, even though I had never been given a clear idea of what it was, as "to save lives, under UN rules of engagement". Under that I analysed the individual tasks and the constraints I was likely to face. We would, for instance, have to sort out medical back-up and be clear on the rules of engagement. The weather was a constraint – winter would begin in mid-November and we would have to get to grips with temperatures of minus 40 degrees. I gave my mission analysis to my officers at 8am the next morning.'

Major General Cordingley believes that mission analysis is a highly effective way of approaching decision-making, and one that the business world could learn from:

'It's a very formal decision-making process, where quite a lot of it is written down. The more often you go through that process the closer you get to being able to come to a quick decision yourself

without having to write down all the factors. I worked out how to make non-intuitive decisions quite quickly and became quite good at taking in information, absorbing the critical factors and working out what to do. I think that's the strength of the system. I became quite confident in my ability to get it right.

'The trouble with modern decision-making, particularly outside the Armed Forces, is that you have an enormous amount of information fed to you. The chief executive or managing director has to be able to recognize the point at which, if he doesn't do something, he is going to lose the opportunity to do whatever he is trying to achieve. If he can do that, he will be able to cut himself off from the information gathering process which, if it goes on for too long, often clouds the issue. I think our training makes us able to recognize that cut-off point.'

In high-risk or fast-moving situations, the greatest comfort for those following the leader is that doubt and indecision is kept to a minimum. Ian Mortimer, who was a key member of Sharkey Ward's squadron during the Falklands War, says that Ward's decisions were not always right, but that the men always appreciated that they knew what they were doing and why they were doing it. 'It would have been much worse for us to be in that situation with a leader who was wishy-washy. If you are the person who actually has to go out and do what they want, and achieve what they are aiming for, what you want is a firm leader who seems to know what they are doing.'

RISK AND THE MILITARY

For leaders in the armed forces, of course, the risks involved in decisions are far greater than anything a business leader will ever face. Colonel Bob Stewart says that while in Bosnia he would plan for risk as carefully as possible with the help of intelligence officers. 'Threat' is 'capability' multiplied by 'intention', he says. Enemy capabilities take time to develop but enemy intention can change rapidly. If there was a chance of an attack against us, I would plan that it might happen. If you expect something hard and it turns out to be softer, that's easy. If you plan for something soft and it turns out to be harder, that's much more difficult.'

Even so, there were inevitably situations where he had to take enormous risks in order to achieve his mission. In common with many other military leaders, Colonel Stewart would choose to take the personal risk himself, rather than put his men in danger. He tells the story of when he had to go out at night to bring a Bosnian Muslim general to a ceasefire meeting:

'We found that our route was blocked by anti-tank mines that had tilt switches on them. All my military life I was told that no-one should touch a mine unless he had a mine clearing officer with the right equipment with him. It's more than your life is worth. But I decided that I had to move the mines in order to get through the roadblock. I had no idea what my chances were of being blown up. But it was a risk I had to take; otherwise I would have failed. So many of the decisions in Bosnia were like that.'

Colonel Stewart's comment is in common with our other military leaders, who all say they were prepared to take enormous risks in order to fulfil their orders. Major General Patrick Cordingley says simply that he was never prepared to accept that his Brigade was doing less than was expected of them, whatever the circumstances. He illustrates this with the story of Desert Rats' assault on Kuwait City during the first Gulf War. His orders were to reach the Basra Highway by 8am on the morning of 28 February 1991:

'There was quite a lot of pressure for us to meet the deadline but we had a number of problems. One was that we were moving in parallel to the Americans, and were not sure where the boundary between them and us lay. The battle group that was travelling alongside them were very concerned that the Americans would open fire on them by mistake. And inevitably they did open fire and the battle group had men wounded. Their very irate commander came on my radio and asked me not to go any further but I said

that we had been told to get on and that was what we were going to do. Under those circumstances you just have to bite the bullet and recognize that it's not going to be all sweetness and light. Everything you've trained for just swings into action.

'At one point during the night we had completed one attack and I could see the advantages of stopping and consolidating, to give everyone a rest and to give the petrol trucks and ammunition lorries a chance to catch up. So I radioed my divisional commander and said we were going to stop for a while. He just said "Well, that's disappointing". I sat there for a few minutes and thought, I'm not prepared to accept that. So I got hold of the planning team and said "we're going to go on". I couldn't accept that we were doing something that was not completely what was expected of us.'

While the military leaders were all committed to the overall mission and objectives, that is not to say that some weren't prepared to break the rules if they felt their men were being put unnecessarily at risk. Sharkey Ward, who commanded 801 Squadron of Sea Harrier jets during the Falklands War, says he effectively tore up the rules of engagement that the pilots were given by the government:

'They were awful, three or four pages about how we couldn't fire unless we were fired on first. I told my pilots that the rules of engagement had been changed and they were now following my rules. I told them to get airborne and shoot everything that moves in a threatening manner and if they got shot down and captured, tell their captors everything because we would change our plans accordingly. If the worst came to the worst, my head would roll for it, not theirs. Then I asked them how they felt and they said, "That's great, boss".'

Sharkey adds that if his squadron was ever asked to do anything that he considered to be an unnecessary risk, he would choose to do it himself rather than send anyone else. 'I'd always ignore directives if I thought someone was trying to kill my pilots by suggesting something stupid. It was part of my view that in a team it's all about loyalty downwards.'

Ian Mortimer, who was Sharkey's wingman during the Falklands, confirms that his commander always led from the front:

'Sharkey would never take risks with his team. He never held back if he thought something was dangerous. He would always do it himself rather than send someone else up. But I have to say that that was partly because he would be livid if he ever missed out on some action!'

RISK AND BUSINESS LEADERS

John Kotter believes that a willingness to take risks is a fundamental feature of modern leaders who are constantly seeking to learn and adapt to the changing environment.[1] Whereas many of their peers become set in their ways, he argues that effective modern leaders show a willingness to push themselves out of their comfort zones.

There are risks involved in almost every business decision but some of our leaders have been prepared to take enormous leaps of faith if they believe in what they are doing. It is a feature, though, that they are generally prepared to take greater personal risks than they are when the organization as a whole is at stake. Sebastian Coe says that he took an enormous personal risk, in terms of his career, when he accepted the role as chair of the London 2012 Olympic and Paralympic Games Bid Committee:

'When I was offered the job we were in fourth place, and not a great fourth place, with less than a year and a half until the final decision. I suppose it would have been very easy to say that I wasn't going to risk it because my personal reputation was at stake. If we had lost I wouldn't be talking to you now about leadership skills, I'd be sitting in front of a select committee explaining why we'd wasted all that money on a failed Olympic bid. But I think life is marginal and good leaders should be prepared to take risks sometimes if they know what they are doing is right.'

In terms of their business decisions, our leaders accept risk as an inevitable part of life, but are generally wary about analysing it. 'In my experience, most of the things that take me by surprise are the things you haven't anticipated,' says Charles Dunstone, co-founder and chief executive of the Carphone Warehouse. 'The one risk that's really under your control as a leader is to make sure that the organization doesn't lose its sense of values, direction and momentum because that's when you're really in trouble.'

Greg Dyke, former director-general of the BBC, takes the view that it is a leader's role to take risks, and to accept the consequences if they fail to pay off. 'If you don't get fired today you'll get fired tomorrow. How many people make retirement age in an organization these days? Virtually none. I think that when you earn £25,000 a year you are entitled to all the protection in the world but when you're taking home £250,000 or more a year you are not entitled to anything. You are taking big money and with that comes risk. That's life.'

There are risks involved in any business but some of our leaders run organizations that are inherently risky, for a variety of reasons. Gail Rebuck, chief executive of Random House publishers, says the company is 'quite openly in the risk business. We publish 1500 books a year and all I ask is that we make more right decisions than wrong ones. But there has to be risk. If everything was safe we wouldn't innovate.'

The autumn of 2005, she adds, was a classic example of the risks that a publishing company must face on a regular basis. During the previous financial year Random House had enjoyed phenomenal success with Dan Brown's *The Da Vinci Code*. Replicating that success, says Rebuck, was near impossible:

> 'That effectively meant a hole in our budget. So we looked at what had sold the previous Christmas when a couple of non-fiction celebrity autobiographies had dominated the market. It was a high risk venture but we decided it was all or nothing. All bets were on the table and I asked everyone to go out and build up a fantastic non-fiction list. We took a lot of expensive risks and there was one

point when I sat there thinking, if we have made more wrong deci-
sions than right ones, we really have had it. Luckily, pretty much
all of our bets paid off. We got six out of the ten top best-sellers in
non-fiction.'

Charles Dunstone makes the point that in a competitive retail environment, companies have to take risks in order to stay ahead. 'If
doing it is the right thing to do, then you just have to get on and make
it happen. Of course there are inherent risks and you could wait
another year until you launched a particular product, but by then
there's no point launching it because the moment is gone. You're
either going to do it or you're not, but you've just got to get on with
it.'

Dunstone has had experience of both sides of the risk equation
during his career. 'The great thing about being in retail is you don't
have to make too many bets,' he says. 'You sell what people want
to buy and if they don't want to buy it, you don't sell it. It's really
simple.' When the company launched its own service, Talk Talk, that
approach had to change somewhat. 'I have a very simple rule, which
is that we won't launch anything on Talk Talk unless someone can
come to me and explain why what we do is unique or better than you
can buy from someone else. If you can buy the exactly same thing
from someone else, then why should we bother?'

One of the company's most successful products in recent years was
the pink Motorola Razr phone which, he says, came from a meeting
one of his marketing staff had with the Motorola company:

'Someone in our marketing department had worked out that 86%
of the people that bought Razr phones were men. The phones were
only available in black or silver at the time. So we asked Motorola
if they could make a pink one. They said they could but they didn't
think people would want them and they would only do it if we
bought 250,000 of them. We agonized about it but took the view
that we would never know until we tried. We sold 600,000 in the
end. But that was a small amount of intuition and a lot of luck.
And a business that's not scared to try things.'

At the other end of the spectrum, the launch of Talk Talk's broadband service (which promised free broadband for life for customers) was a risk that failed, initially at least, to pay off. The company suffered a mauling in the press when it was unable to keep up with the demand from customers. Dunstone says he has learned from the experience:

> *'Talk Talk was an interesting lesson because it was the first time things had really gone wrong. To be fair, whatever we've done in the past, even if it didn't work out quite how we expected, we could usually fix it with a week of working all night. This time we started something that was so big that we couldn't do that. For the first time, my slightly gung-ho, "we'll figure it out" methodology really hit the rocks. The trouble is that doing something like that is very binary. One day you're not doing it and the next day you are. It's hard to test the reaction to it and your ability to cope with it. You don't know that the engine will run dry until you start it. We did masses of work to check that we were ready and the processes worked but we ended up with massive demand that we couldn't cope with, and some processes that had gaps in them. But in spite of what [the press] put us through, it was the right thing to do and I'd do it again.'*

Some of the most successful products or campaigns undertaken by companies have started life as a risky proposition. Greg Dyke says that the free digital television service, Freeview, was the result of an informal discussion he had with two fellow BBC executives. 'People have said that it was a brave decision that worked but it wasn't brave, it was just a calculated risk. The trouble with many public sector organizations is that the downside when something goes wrong is often far too great and as a result they fail to take risks.'

Martin Glenn says that the phenomenally successful Walkers crisps advertising campaign, which starred Gary Lineker, was considered one of his biggest risks while running the division:

'We had a great business at Walkers but a lousy brand. It really wasn't known outside the Midlands. So we knew that we needed a really disruptive advertising campaign. What hadn't been done in the UK at that point was to look at the crisp campaigns that worked in other developed markets, which tended to be based around the ideas of irresistibility and celebrity. So we briefed the ad agency and they came up with the idea of Lineker and No More Mr Nice Guy, which was bang on. Selling the idea to my American boss was a struggle but I always thought it was going to be huge. I never really considered it to be a risk.'

Invariably, some risks do not pay off. In the next chapter we look at the mistakes our leaders have made during their career and how they turned adversity into opportunity.

WHAT LEADERS REALLY DO:

- Know, often instinctively, when the time is right to make a decision
- Are not afraid to delay a decision
- Are able to weigh up facts quickly and identify important information
- Accept risk as part of life and the price you pay for innovation
- Accept ultimate responsibility for decisions taken
- Embrace calculated risks.

---

[1] *Leading Change*, p 183

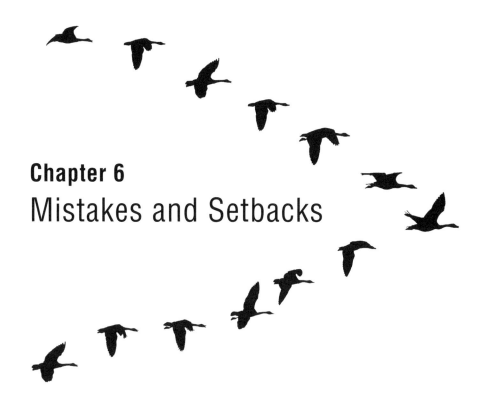

Chapter 6
Mistakes and Setbacks

The problem (in America today) is not that we fail, it is that we don't risk failing enough.

Phil Knight, Nike

As we have seen, our leaders generally take the view that risk is an everyday part of their organization and has to be accepted. In the same spirit, our leaders view mistakes as an occupational hazard. Irrespective of the type of organization, a common trait among our leaders was that they accept that honest mistakes happen and do not dwell on them – unless, that is, the mistakes turn out to be persistent and recurring.

Sir Clive Woodward says he tells the players he works with that 'it's not a perfect world. You can do everything humanly possible and you can still lose. As long as you can look at each other afterwards, shake hands and know that you did everything possible, life's great. That's how I have always done it.'

Martin Johnson, who was captain of the England rugby team during Woodward's tenure, adds that it was a feature of the team that everyone was prepared to admit to their mistakes and then move on. 'If any of us made mistakes we would put our hand up and say so. We had a very honest team in that way. We could all give and take critical feedback. If something wasn't going right, we would always say so.' Importantly in pressurized situations, the team also had the ability to pick themselves up quickly and move on if they made a mistake. The most pressurized situation the team ever faced was, of course, the rugby World Cup final. Johnson tells of a point during the first half when Ben Kay dropped the ball metres from Australia's try line when he was seconds away from scoring:

'He knocked the ball on and we ended up with a scrum. Someone was injured at that point so there was a pause in the game. It was obvious that he knew what he had done and was desperately trying not to think about it too much. I looked at him and said, "You alright?" and he just said "Yep," but I could see that he was fine. He wasn't wide-eyed or panicky. He said after the game that he had used that mistake as a focus, which is the best thing that you can do. And I could see that – he was concentrating totally on what was going to happen next. That's important. It was our whole mindset. We don't worry about what has happened or about what we can't control. It's gone. Just worry about what you can do next.'

Martin Glenn, chief executive of Birds Eye Iglo, has similar views to Woodward when it comes to mistakes and as a result, says that his employees find him approachable as a leader:

'People feel it fairly easy to give me bad news. In my view you have to see them as a learning opportunity, unless they are sequential. Everyone makes mistakes but some things I do persistently badly, just because they are a weak area of my game. The types of mis-

takes are important. I'm a big believer that most honest mistakes should be treated as learning opportunities. The mistakes that are caused by an underlying personality deficit, or because someone hasn't tried or has done sloppy work, have to be confronted. I can't forgive lack of effort. It saps energy from an organization.'

Some of our leaders say that they have learned not to dwell on mistakes through the experience earlier in their career of making errors themselves. Gail Rebuck, chief executive of Random House says that all of her bosses were understanding when she made mistakes earlier in her career. 'I've always made mistakes and all of my bosses have been very indulgent and said look, you've beaten yourself up about this enough. Just learn from it and move on. That is such a valuable lesson, it really is.'

Major General Patrick Cordingley argues that he, as a young officer training during the Cold War, had the 'luxury of failure' in the knowledge that there were very few serious consequences if he got something wrong. He, along with all of our leaders, believes that it is vital to analyse failures:

'I was fortunately brought up by a lot of very good commanders who were more interested in your errors than they were in your successes, because they felt that everyone learnt something from an error. A good leader will understand that there are advantages in people making mistakes because there is a sporting chance that you will learn a lot more from making a mistake than you will from getting it right – provided someone points it out to you in a friendly manner and takes you through what went wrong.'

Our leaders felt it was important to acknowledge mistakes when they happen, but not to apportion blame. 'The most important thing is not to try and pretend that it hasn't happened,' says Lord Inge. 'You have to be honest about it and say, we've screwed up here. Then you have to look at why it happened and what you are going to do about it. If the mistake was the result of a lack of knowledge or a lack of necessary assets, you have to see what you can do about that.'

'If I'm upset about something I get on the phone very quickly, talk to the guy or girl in question and move on,' says Kevin Roberts of Saatchi & Saatchi. 'We never blame and we never follow up. It's just, boom, done with.' Colonel Bob Stewart employed similar tactics during his career in the Army and argues that in the business world, management is often too quick to condemn someone for making a wrong decision, which in turn destroys an organization's ability to create and innovate. 'I used to say to my officers, "Make your decision, I will back it. Right or wrong, I will back you. I won't let you down. And hopefully at least 51% of your decisions will be the correct ones."'

Martin Glenn says that he learned the hard way that if something is not working, there is no shame in going back to change earlier decisions. He feels that he made some major misjudgements while attempting to merge businesses within Pepsico UK:

> *'I was given a brief to run the business and came to the view very quickly that I should merge them very hard and get rid of three general managers. It would create some ugliness for a while but I felt it was the right decision. I overestimated my ability to manage the integration of the kind of issues that I and my team had found very easy to sort out in the Walkers business. I convinced myself that I was superman and that I understood the Walkers business inside and out and therefore could understand these three much smaller businesses in a heartbeat. I misunderstood the complexity of them. If I could rewind the tape I'd do it very differently. I'd allow myself more time to do what I'm good at, which is helicoptering and looking at the big picture. From the outside, everything looked fine but it made me tired and there was a personal cost to it as well as the physical strain and wear and tear. It was probably a factor in my deciding to cut links with Pepsico.'*

There is a strong feeling among the leaders that when something does go wrong, it is important for the organization to admit the mistake and for the leader to accept ultimate responsibility. 'I don't tend to brood over mistakes, I think about them and then move on,' says Dame Stella Rimington. 'But when things go wrong you have to take responsibility. Responsibility moves upward in a good organization. It's the antithesis of the blame culture.'

Greg Dyke takes the same view and says that while he was director-general, the BBC introduced a new system for expenses that, it soon became clear, was not working. 'It was a disaster. It was clearly wrong,' he says. 'So I just put out an email saying sorry, we got it wrong. We'll start again. Management generally have a terrible habit of failing to admit when they've made a mistake. We all screw up. If you admit it, everyone likes you.' He adds that he has first-hand experience of this, as a consumer rather than as a leader:

'I was on a Virgin plane, ready to take off in Hong Kong on our way to London and the plane was stopped on the runway because the computer went down. It was really important that I got back to London but there was a 14-hour delay before we could finally take off, so I was really pissed off with Virgin. Most of us were. So what does Richard Branson do? He rang us to say he was sorry. And that's what people are talking about now, not about being stuck in Hong Kong for 14 hours because the airline were rubbish, but about how the chief executive of the airline rang them personally to apologize.'

From time to time an organization will face a crisis of one description or another and the way it is handled, in terms of both internal and external communication, can have a profound effect on the reputation of the business and the morale of its employees. The leaders we spoke to generally take the view that honesty is the best policy when it comes to public mistakes and that it is important to accept responsibility for them.

The launch of Carphone Warehouse's Talk Talk broadband service was, says Charles Dunstone, one of the greatest tests of his leadership ability. The service attracted an enormous level of media condemnation when the company failed to keep up with demand from consumers. Dunstone says that while the launch of the service was done for all the right reasons, it was perceived as a massive mistake by the company because of the intense media coverage that it generated:

> *'There's no doubt that what we've done with the broadband service has damaged our brand and we will have to recover that. That's the price you pay [for taking a risk]. But if you are doing the right thing for your customers and your people are trying as hard as they can to get it right, you can't expect more than that. We are trying to make a very genuine offer that is substantially cheaper than anyone else in the marketplace. We stumbled in the delivery of that but we had the best possible motives and that matters to our organization. We were not trying to exploit people or make a profit out of them. It wasn't a betrayal of our company values, it was a mess up.'*

Dunstone says that from the outset he took the decision to be honest with customers and the press about the difficulties with the service, but the resulting press coverage has made him think carefully about how his company communicates with the press and outsiders. 'It was a complete bun fight,' he says. 'We got ourselves in a terrible mess and that's when you've got to try and keep the people within the company together as well as trying to keep our customers tolerant and patient with us. In other words you've got to manage the internal and external world.'

Potential PR crises are often the sternest test of a leader's ability and history does suggest that, faced with a situation such as the Talk Talk experience, companies that promptly and honestly admit their mistakes are more likely to ride out the PR storm. Generally, customers are more willing to forgive what they see as an honest mistake and immediate and truthful communication also gives less time for the inevitable (and often far more damaging) rumours to develop.

On balance, Dunstone feels that it was the right decision for Carphone Warehouse to be open and honest about the difficulties with the Talk Talk broadband service:

> *'We've had huge debates about this because we were brutally honest about what was happening and so we had our fair share of*

a kicking in the media. As we learned more and more about the situation we realized that we weren't in much more of a mess than many of our competitors, but they were keeping their heads below the parapet. We ended up getting all of the media attention because [the press] are inherently lazy and if you are the obvious people for them to target, that is what they will do. With hindsight it's a very interesting debate and it's impossible to know whether we were right to be so honest and open. It was certainly the right approach internally and it was certainly the right approach with our customers and at the end of the day, they have to be your priority. But it did mean that we were the media's whipping boy.'

LEARNING FROM EXPERIENCE

No leader can ever claim to have gone through their career without making a single mistake. Our leaders were happy to admit to setbacks of their own and say that they were an important learning experience. As Jack Welch says, you learn more about yourself from your failures than you do from your successes. Once again, this ties in with John Kotter's observation of leaders. Modern leaders, he says, exhibit ability for humble self-reflection and a willingness to assess both successes and failures, and learn from both.

Sir Clive Woodward says that he learned from his experience as coach to the British Lions team on their less-than-successful tour to New Zealand 2005:

'The problem I had with the Lions was that I had too much time to think about it. We had eight months to plan a four-week tour and I ended up putting my eight years of experience with England into a week's preparation with the players. The England players I knew very well but I was working with other players I hadn't met before. All of the stuff I brought in just blew them away. I should have been more realistic about what we were doing. I gave the players far too much information and I used too many people. In trying to pull a team together from four nations in less than four weeks while still playing opposition and then play a fresh, well-prepared team at its

best, I learnt that you need to keep things as simple as possible and even then, playing away from home, it's a big ask.'

Gail Rebuck of Random House says that her biggest mistake came out of an inherited problem, although she adds that that 'is beside the point. It happened on my watch'. The problem lay in the company's distribution warehouse, which (after a new warehouse system was introduced) was failing to function efficiently and was resulting in delays and lost orders. Rebuck was a relatively new CEO and says that her first mistake was to let the operational side of the company sort the mess out because distribution was not part of her skills set:

'I brought in some advisers and people from the US business to have a look, but it still wasn't getting sorted. My big mistake was that I was frightened that I wouldn't have anything to contribute to the solution. I didn't think that I knew enough about the technical side of the business and because of that I didn't show enough leadership early on.

'It was only when it got worse and everyone was complaining to me that I thought that I had better take a lead. I started going out to our distribution centre, which was near Colchester, every morning. I would get up at 3am and be there for the first shift. It was a nightmare time and even today my kids still remember it from their childhood.

'I had to understand how it all worked so when I got there I said to the management team that I was a book, I had just arrived and I wanted to get to WHSmith. Please take me through the process. It was only by doing that, by admitting complete ignorance, that I actually got to understand what the problem was. It wasn't a technical problem at all, it was a human operational problem and it was actually not resolvable because the whole stock location system had become corrupted. I realized at that point that there was no getting away from the fact that we had to close the place down, do a stock take, clean up all the computer records, have a

massive new training session for all the staff and then start again. We also had to replace several of the management team. What I learnt from that was that you should always own up to something you don't understand because it is only when you get to understand it that you can actually make a contribution to its solution.'

Considering that so many leaders operate under a constant media spotlight, it is hardly surprising that many of the mistakes and difficult situations faced by our leaders during their career are centred around the press. One of the most difficult moments during Major General Patrick Cordingley's career came while he was stationed in the Gulf before the liberation of Kuwait. While briefing a group of defence correspondents from the national newspapers a few weeks before the attack on Kuwait began, he was asked what level of casualties the British public should be prepared for. His answer was that it was inevitable that when two armies the size of the forces in the Gulf went to war, there would be considerable casualties. He added that clearly the majority of casualties would be on the losing side, which would be Iraq. Another officer estimated that the casualty rate would be 15%. The resulting headline in a London newspaper was that the public should 'Prepare for a Bloodbath'. A few days after the resulting PR storm exploded, Major General Cordingley went to Bahrain for a previously arranged few days' break:

'My boss was keen that the senior commanders should remain as refreshed as possible for the moment of battle. So I ended up in a hotel suite in Bahrain for two days. That was a huge mistake because all of my thoughts were with my soldiers back in the desert. Why should I be sitting in a hotel when they were out there? And of course the other problem was the newspapers – the Sunday papers had just come out and I had time to read all of them. They all had an opinion, some supportive, some not.

'The soldiers were well aware of what had gone on and they didn't mind in the slightest. But I was more concerned about what their wives and girlfriends would think. The one place I didn't need to be

was sitting in a hotel room in Bahrain. Once I was back with them
I was fine. It was an interesting lesson. If you do get yourself into
a spot of bother, don't isolate yourself from your friends because
that's when you really need them.'

Sebastian Coe also faced a serious PR crisis while chairman of the
London 2012 Olympic and Paralympic Games Bid Committee.
Three months before the winning bid was announced, the London
team announced what it called the National Olympics Charter and
Athletes Charter during an International Olympics Committee
(IOC) meeting in Berlin. As part of the initiative, the Committee
was promising free rail travel for athletes for two weeks before and
during the Games should London win the bid, as well as discounts at
a number of shops and restaurants. It also offered money pledges to
each national Olympic committee, to be used to support UK training
camps in the run-up to the Games. Coe says, though, that the idea
'was not spun very well' and the result was a series of press articles
that alleged that the London team was attempting to offer induce-
ments that could sway the IOC members. The following day, the IOC
President asked the London team to withdraw the offer. Coe takes
up the story:

'It was a pretty horrible weekend. We were accused of bribery and
people said we had destroyed London's chances of winning the
bid. A Daily Telegraph journalist had gone on the radio on the
Sunday and said that my director of communications should be
sacked. I came into the office on the Monday morning and it was
clear that everyone was very nervous and people were beginning
to say, "It wasn't my fault". So I collected the team together in a
room and said I was sure they had seen the press coverage over the
weekend but I was just going to say two things. First, if anyone was
going to be sacked that day it was going to be me and second, I was
not having anyone looking for a lifebelt or escape route.

'I said my door would be open for the next hour and a half and
anyone could come and say whatever they wanted but after that, I

never wanted to hear the subject raised again. It was over and we needed to move on and fight on. That brought everyone together. Sometimes you just need to draw a line under something. You can have the most forensic discussion about what went wrong and if it's my fault I will hold my hands up but that's where it finishes. It's internal and once it's all agreed we don't keep revisiting it every hour with another accusation.'

Some of our leaders have faced setbacks that are less public but nevertheless painful. Heather Rabbatts, chair of Millwall Football Club and former chief executive of Lambeth council, said that she learned a valuable lesson when she allowed her judgement of a close colleague to be clouded.

'This was someone who was quite a senior member of my team who became quite a close friend. It was a difficult time for me anyway because I had had a bereavement in my family and this person was very supportive to me personally during all of that. But because I did like her I think my judgement was clouded and I started to give her too much of the benefit of the doubt when some problems began to be uncovered in her department. Although she was a great director of the department, she was not as steely as she should have been and that eventually led to a massive problem that we had to deal with. In the end she resigned. I learned two lessons from that. One was that when you are running a big organization where you are quite far away from the front line, it's difficult to know when things are not working properly and you have to trust the people who are working for you. It also reinforced my sense of how you should manage your team and how close you should let them get to you and you to them. I'm normally pretty good at judging people and knowing what their limits are but on this occasion, I lost some of my judgement. I should have been tougher earlier.'

ANALYSING FAILURE AND SUCCESS

All of our leaders understand that while mistakes do happen, it is important to understand why they happen, and to learn from the experience. Charles Dunstone of the Carphone Warehouse takes the view that a leader should never assume that failure is an isolated event:

> 'We had this thing with Talk Talk that if someone said, "That was just a one off", you knew that it wasn't. It's never a one-off. If a customer didn't get a letter or got the wrong letter, you can guarantee that there will be other people in the same situation. Sometimes it will be systematic, and sometimes something else will have happened. Every time, you have to just pull on the reins and find out what actually happened.'

Sir Clive Woodward says that 'feedback is vitally important to any business', but took the same view to every game played by the England team while he was in charge:

> 'I gave them immediate feedback within five or ten minutes of the final whistle and collected everyone together in the changing room. But to be honest the only reason I did that was because of the media. It was important that no-one spoke to the media until I had spoken to the team, so when we do speak to the press we are coming across as a collective. You can get the major messages across in that five or ten minutes. With coaches' meetings, though, I think you need 24 hours to allow the players to calm down and reflect on the match, and then they get the really detailed feedback. I believe in talking things through and not rushing back onto the training pitch until you have done that.

> 'People often see feedback as negative. It's not. Feedback can be incredibly positive and it should be positive. For most of the meetings, we would have won the game. But if we had lost, the meeting was the same, not emotional but analytical. We went through team

performance and individual performance using videos and data.
The coaches put a lot of work in between the game on Saturday
and Monday morning and the players knew that.'

Woodward adds that it is equally important for a company, team or
other organization to analyse its success as well as its failures, since
it is the successes you should be looking to repeat and emulate, and
not the failures. Too often, he says, when a company wins a new client
or completes a successful deal, the team heads off to the pub to celebrate. But while celebration may be good for morale, the company
should also be analysing what went right on that particular occasion.
If it does not know for sure, how can it hope to repeat it in the future?
(Sebastian Coe's view of this is that if you do not know why you succeeded, it must have been an accident.) Martin Glenn says that he
borrowed this view from Woodward and implemented it in his own
business. 'It is important in any complex business to codify things and
saying that something is worth taking seriously because it has worked
here for these reasons.'

Gail Rebuck agrees, but says that part of the reason why she
encourages her team to analyse its successes as well as its failures
is because only looking at the failures can dent an organization's
morale:

> *'To begin with – we only had post mortems of book failures, to try*
> *and understand what went wrong and that was just too depress-*
> *ing. So we also began to look at our successes, and to share best*
> *practice. It meant that if we looked at something that failed at least*
> *we could then look at something that was successful alongside it,*
> *and people didn't go away on a downer after spending half an hour*
> *looking at all of those books that we should never have bought.*
> *That worked quite well because everyone felt much lighter and*
> *more committed and enthused, and not so fearful of the process.*
> *And I also found that people were more willing to talk intelligently*
> *about failure if it was within the context of success, which was*
> *interesting.'*

Overall, the leaders we spoke to adopted what could be seen as a remarkably relaxed attitude towards mistakes. The reality, though, is that all recognized mistakes as an inevitable part of their role and are determined to treat any that happen as a learning opportunity rather than an event that could ultimately stifle the organization's ability to innovate.

WHAT LEADERS REALLY DO:

- Accept mistakes as inevitable
- See honest mistakes as learning opportunities
- Do not punish bad news
- Forgive everything except lack of effort
- Admit mistakes and accept ultimate responsibility for them
- Acknowledge mistakes and move on, unless they are sequential
- Are not afraid to return to previous decisions if they need correcting
- Analyse successes as well as failures.

Chapter 7
Change Management

The task of a leader is to take people from where they are to where they have not been.

Henry Kissinger

Change management is considered to be a key characteristic of leadership by many of the leading academics and leadership writers. For John Kotter, leadership is all about change: 'What leaders really do is prepare an organization for change and help them cope as they struggle through it,' he says.[1]

There are two distinct but related elements to change. First, there is the ongoing change that inevitably surrounds organizations, much of which is beyond their control. As John Kotter says, the business world has become more competitive and more volatile over recent

years, thanks to deregulation, technological development, international competition and a host of other factors. 'The net result is that
doing what was done yesterday, or doing it 5% better, is no longer a
formula for success. Major changes are more and more necessary to
survive and compete.' This leads to the second element, the specific
change initiatives that are introduced by leaders in order to address
a changing environment or prepare an organization for the future.
These may be planned, or introduced in response to crisis.

All organizations, whatever their business, operate in a constantly
changing environment. The only variant is the pace of change.
Charles Dunstone, co-founder and chief executive of the Carphone
Warehouse, says that his is a company that is 'used to surprises', given
the breakneck speed of technological developments in its industry.
'Your core values should remain the same but leadership is about
preparing an organization for change,' he says. 'You have to make
sure that your organization is adaptable to changing circumstances
and constantly reinventing itself.'

'Change doesn't just happen, it goes on all the time,' agrees Dame
Stella Rimington, who oversaw a wide-ranging culture change
programme while director-general of MI5. 'I don't think that was
something we fully understood at the time. Looking back, we thought
when all this change is over we can get on with our core job. You have
to create an organization that understands that the old days are over
and does not resent new situations but can adapt to them The real
problem is that if you don't change at the right speed, then you get a
crisis, and we had a couple of those at MI5. If you see those as opportunities, which I think you have to, you continue to move forward.'

Ron Dennis of McLaren makes the point that it is far easier to
lead a change programme out of failure than it is in a successful
organization. 'If you are already successful you tend to hold your
breath and think that you need to be very careful about what you
change. But history shows that very often, that is not what happens.
You can make a change and it triggers failure but if you don't change,
failure is inevitable as well. You are caught between a rock and a
hard place.' Lord Inge characterizes this by saying that good leaders
always have a feel for what he calls 'the art of the possible'.

The best leaders are able to recognize – and sometimes predict – the changes that are ahead. That may sometimes mean persuading the organization to change its message or direction when, on the surface, it seems to be operating successfully. 'That's a lonely call for a CEO,' says Martin Glenn, 'to make a decision to fix something because the rules for success may not be working any more.'

Glenn says that one of the last decisions he made while President of the Walkers snack foods business was to encourage the organization to tackle the issue of healthy eating. 'It was clear to me that the whole debate around obesity was going to have an impact on the Walkers business,' he says. 'Our success meant that were going to be a poster child for the issue. The businesses I have worked with have generally been good about joining together when under attack, but there is a danger that too much of that can make you inflexible and unable to see what is going on.' Glenn says he learnt this important lesson from Steve Rightman, who was chief executive during his time at Pepsico:

'Steve said that our mantra at Pepsico had always been that there are no junk foods, just junk diets. But even if it was true, he said, people no longer believed that and Pepsico was at the centre of the debate about diet and what counts as a good product. He felt that the company should take a leadership role by making it easier for people who wanted better-for-you versions of our snackfood products. That idea went down really badly in the business at first, because it was seen as a chink in our armour to the outside world.

'So one of the last things I did at Walkers was to try to engage with our customers in a different way. We used a political pollster and asked how Walkers would be doing if it was a political party. We learnt a whole load of stuff: that the brand was popular but it was felt that the irresistibility factor was a problem. We weren't helping out busy mums. They wanted us to help them provide balance. That led us to completely reformulate our cooking oil. We knew we could blend the cooking oils with a lower saturated fat version

and people wouldn't notice the difference, it would just be more expensive. So we decided to go ahead and figure out how to pay for it later. We also needed to advertise in a different way and engage in the debate, because we were in danger of being demonized over the issue. It became like a mini political campaign. How the business is seen in the wider world is absolutely critical.'

In this chapter leaders talk about how they introduced and managed change programmes, and the challenges they faced along the way. How do they communicate change within the organization and, critically, bring employees onside? How do they judge the right pace of change for their organization? And how do they keep the momentum for change?

Heather Rabbatts compares the process of managing change to 'spinning plates, juggling a series of different elements'. In common with other leaders, she argues that the key to a successful change initiative is 'getting the metrics right between having sufficient critical presence of change, so people believe that it is possible, and managing the longer-running changes that will ultimately put the organization on a better footing'.

Martin Glenn, says that change is 'an organic process, not a scientific one'. His comment that change 'needs a massive amount of sponsorship and ownership from the person at the top' is a sentiment that all of the leaders would agree with. If the leader is not fully and enthusiastically committed to change, there is little hope that the rest of the organization will follow. Sue Campbell, chair of UK Sport, stresses the enormous amount of energy it takes a leader to see through a successful change programme: 'You can't make people change, you can only change the environment and expectations. You have to take people with you every step of the way. It has to be a shared process, winning together.'

WHY DO MOST CHANGE INITIATIVES FAIL?

It is widely recognized that most change initiatives adopted by management – it is estimated as many as 75% – fail, for a variety of reasons.

Ron Dennis of McLaren believes that change programmes often fail simply because management form a complex model for change but then fail to remember that people are equally complex. 'We are quirky beings and we have personalities,' he says. 'If change initiatives fail it is because as the model moves down the organization, management does not have the ability to adapt and change it to accommodate the strengths and weaknesses of the people who are being asked to implement it.'

Martin Glenn, who oversaw a far-reaching change programme while President of Walkers between 1998 and 2003, argues that the biggest difficulty with implementing change initiatives is that 'people don't like change'. For that reason, he says, it is vital that the reasons for any change programme are clearly and consistently explained. 'You get the best out of people and systems when there is a real clarity about how things work,' he says. 'If you throw a spanner in that works you have to be clear about what the upside is.' Glenn says that he is 'not gung-ho about change, *per se*' but while he is cautious, he does not necessarily believe in the maxim that if it ain't broke, don't fix it. 'The important thing is to be careful and do it properly – don't dabble. People need to understand what the broad objective is, and that requires the leader to say very early on that he thinks that there is a problem or an opportunity if we do something differently, here is the rough time frame and here is what I'm certain about and what I'm not certain about. The leader has to really own the change process.'

Glenn adds that the 'command and control' approach to change can still work in the modern environment, but it is unnecessarily hard work. The leaders unanimously agree that no change initiative is going to work unless the leader is able to get the people onside. 'Half of the problem,' says Gail Rebuck of Random House, 'is that people might pay lip service to the idea and then do exactly the opposite to what is required.' She cites the example of the new management system – discussed in the previous chapter – that was put in place in the company's distribution centre shortly before she was appointed as CEO of Random House:

'The new warehouse management system was much more sophisticated than the previous system, which had always worked well, and it required a change in working practices. But no-one had really thought about [the implications of] that. I think the workforce just thought well, we've always done it this way and we have always made it work by doing it this way, so I'm not going to do it any differently. That, of course, was a complete disaster and caused a meltdown in our distribution system. You have to do your best to explain change to people and get them on board. In the end, it was a management communication and training failure, classic stuff.'

Greg Dyke, whose strength as a leader lies in his ability to empathize with his staff, agrees that 'you can only bring about change if you have your people onside', but makes the additional point that it is important to identify why a change initiative might be important to employees. At the BBC, he says, he always talked in terms of how change would result in the BBC producing better programmes. 'If you have the same aim as everyone else, people will let you bring about change even if it's unpopular.'

Heather Rabbatts, who oversaw a massive programme of reform while chief executive of the Borough of Lambeth, says that one of the most difficult elements in keeping people onside lies in managing expectations about what the change programme can achieve. 'Managing expectations is very difficult, partly because as soon as people recognize that you have made one step forward, they add something else to the list. What's next? You have to keep people focused on what you said you were going to do, while also reminding them that the glass is half full and not half empty because people tend to forget what you have done and concentrate on the problems that haven't been solved yet. And you have to keep reminding them of the journey because everyone, rightly so, lives in the present.'

COMMUNICATING CHANGE

Implementing a successful change initiative requires communication, and lots of it. Communication is often identified as an area that sabotages change programmes, not necessarily because it is mismanaged or imprecise, but because management underestimates how often the message has to be repeated before it filters through to all parts of the organization. There is a danger, says Greg Dyke, that by the time the message is heard and understood by the last employee, management has long moved on to something else (that is, to them, more interesting). As Martin Glenn says, 'It's little and often, not long and loud. You've got to keep saying it, like a broken record, even though you might be bored to death of it.'

When she was appointed chief executive of Random House, Gail Rebuck says that 'The company had been through so many changes by that stage that people didn't like the idea of change. I knew that not only did there have to be big dramatic change, we also had to respond to the dynamic external situation, which meant that strategy could not be fixed but had to flow, part of an evolving process.' The fact that Random House was a relatively small company at the time, though, meant that Rebuck was in a position to communicate her future plans to everyone at once. 'I used a powerpoint presentation to explain exactly what the problem was, why we were losing money and what we had to do about it. It meant that some jobs would go but I explained that if we did that, we would grow and grow and be successful. They could see that having five or six people in the organization all providing the same service function for different imprints wasn't a particularly good idea.'

When Sir Clive Woodward was appointed coach of the England rugby union team in 1997, part of his task was to manage the transition of the team from the amateur to the professional era. He says that the key to any change initiative is communication, both talking to people and listening. 'There's no shortcut to it,' he says, 'you've got to have lots and lots of meetings.'

Sir Clive adds that a change programme can be complicated by people outside of the organization – particularly one that invites as much press comment as the England rugby team – who will have their own views. 'I find that most people without exception will want to embrace change but some are scared of it, that it might not happen correctly, or are scared of ridicule or of the media. All of those things hold them back. So if you take all of that away, and say that you will handle it all, everyone gets excited about the idea of change.' Sir Clive gives the example of when he gave all of the players laptop computers, early on in his time as manager:

> *'My vision was that if you lead in technology, the chances are that you are going to lead elsewhere. But the idea of the players using laptops and getting their training schedules by email in 1997 was just ridiculed. One of the headlines called me the mad professor, and asked why I wasn't giving them raw meat instead. Half of the players didn't know how to use a computer at that stage anyway. So I said that I was going to email all of them with the team announcement an hour before I released it to the press. The press said I was a computer geek but that wasn't the point. I was trying to get them to use the computers. All of the players use them now, and download matches to watch. It was the way ahead.'*

The English cricket team went through a similar transition from the amateur to professional era. When Nasser Hussain was named captain of the team in 1999, elements of the amateur culture were still prevalent within the team. During his captaincy the fitness training regime was improved, the support system while the team was on tour was upgraded and central contracts were introduced for the players. Nasser says, though, that the culture change had to be led by the key players through example. 'As Steve Bull says, it is about getting the right people in the right seats on the bus. You have to put people in the team who in themselves will change the culture. It's not always about the coach or the captain communicating the changes. We tried to get the right people into the team who would lead the way, like Michael Vaughan and Marcus Trescothick. If Vaughan said at the end of a day's training, "we're all going to the gym", we would all go to the gym.'

It is perhaps easier for a leader to initiate a change programme if they are themselves the representative of something new. For leaders who have been part of the organization for years, the challenges can be more significant. Dame Stella Rimington oversaw a groundbreaking programme to introduce more transparency in MI5 during her tenure, but says that the fact that she had been with the organisation made it easier for her to understand the difficulties it would face. She says she got the message across at MI5 by 'recruiting supporters' outside of the organization and by continually explaining and presenting the options within the organization. 'That's the only way I know how to do it, by communicating and listening. I tried to persuade by explaining the advantages and the disadvantages [of becoming more transparent] and in the end most people bought into it.'

Dame Stella has also seen a change management programme from the other side of the fence, since earlier in her career a new Director-General, Sir Anthony Duff, was brought in from outside of the organization at a time when MI5 was considered to be in disarray after a series of crises, such as the publication of Peter Wright's book *Spycatcher*, had damaged its internal and external reputation:

'His style was completely different from the style of the people that had gone before. The first thing he did was to go around the entire organization to meet everyone and listen to the issues that they raised. He understood the importance of listening and trying to get the measure of this organization he had been brought in to lead. I thought that was a very admirable thing and exactly the right thing to do at that moment. It was so different from what had gone on before, when we hardly ever saw the leaders and there was no real sense of them listening or even wanting to know what the people lower down the organization thought.'

CULTURE CHANGE

Instilling a new culture within an organization is perhaps one of the most challenging tasks a leader can undertake. Three of our leaders – Greg Dyke at the BBC, Heather Rabbatts at the London Borough of Lambeth and Sue Campbell at UK Sport – introduced far-reaching culture change programmes in their own organizations, in two cases because the organization was effectively in crisis.

In Heather Rabbatts' case, she already knew the scale of the challenge facing her since she had been appointed chief executive of the Borough of Lambeth after replying to an advertisement that claimed it was 'the worst job in local government'. An official report into the state of the borough had described it as being in 'an appalling financial and administrative mess with non-existent or incompetent management'. When she joined the council, Rabbatts freely admits that many people working within the organization felt it was beyond redemption, because they had been told so frequently that it was. She was also aware that any change at the organization would be carried out very much under the gaze of the public and the press. The first step for Rabbatts was to persuade the people within the organization that change for the better was a real possibility:

'I think in any organization there are always good, hardworking people. There are some people that you need to deal with, but the overwhelming majority want to be better. The key at Lambeth was to try and instil a sense of belief that it could be different, even though various people had promised the same thing in the past and failed. But because Lambeth was being written about in the papers on a daily basis, we couldn't just carry out a nice little rebranding exercise, close the curtains and then reveal the new shape of the organization. So we had to get our people to believe that it could change and believe it could be different while they were still reading bad headlines. That was the biggest challenge, to get a sense of momentum in what was essentially a bureaucracy and therefore not particularly responsive to change.

'For me the secret was absolutely being as visible as possible, going out there and talking to people. I didn't use any of the strategies that the management books talk about but the metaphor that I used when I talked about change was to imagine that they were watching a bank of television screens, some of which were playing comedies, some dramas, some documentaries and so on. The idea I was trying to get across was that if you are going to shift a complex organization, you have to simultaneously intervene at different levels.'

Sue Campbell was appointed Reform Chair of UK Sport in 2004. She says her appointment was the most serious test of her leadership skills throughout her career, since it was one thing to build an organization from scratch and have people choose to work with you but quite another to go into a building where the organizational culture was not one you were familiar with and where no-one knew what you stood for or why you were there. Her first meeting with the employees at the company suggested that they saw her as a threat, a short-term reformer who would seek to change everything. She takes up the story:

'I realized that this was going to be a long journey but I started by getting to know the people. I walked around the building, sat on people's desks and said, "Who are you? Tell me what you do. Do you care if we get this right? What stops you doing your job better?" And I discovered that there were a lot of passionate people here with a lot of ability, who were being weighed down by process rather than focused on outcomes. So I tried to give them greater freedom and responsibility – I got rid of many of the committees, for example. Someone came to my door and said, "You got rid of my committee," and I said yes, I had. He said, "So who makes the decisions now?" and I said, you do. He thought for a bit and said, "What if I get it wrong?" and I said that's easy, you get sacked. He laughed and walked away. Then he came back a few minutes later and said, "You weren't serious, were you?" And I said no, I wasn't.

'There are a number of conditions that I believe create a positive environment. The first is creating a sense of belonging for everyone in the company. You have to have a sense that you are respected and valued for what you do and who you are. Another important area is role models, someone people can look up to. We all need them, and it can be the person sitting at the desk next to you. It is also really important to have fun and enjoyment in your work place and a sense of achievement in your job. Developing, support- ing and rewarding, curiosity and creativity can also provide new and exciting developments for individuals and for the company. If you can create those conditions in an organization, you create change.'

Heather Rabbatts is now executive chair of Millwall Football Club, which was, when she was appointed, another organization with a repu- tation problem. When Rabbatts accepted the post of vice-chairman, the club had no manager in place and half of its players were out of contract. Her priority, she says, was to instil management methods in an organization that was unfamiliar with modern business techniques:

'The first priority was to sort out the manager and the players' contracts but the second was to modernize the club. With a few exceptions, football is still overwhelmingly run like a small sweet shop and so I have tried to put in place all of the modern manage- ment methods to try to run it more effectively. We are listed on the market and need to operate in a much more professional and open way. That means new ticketing systems and changes to the catering and a new look and feel to our marketing campaign. So we've said that we've got the team now, so let's start to modernize the infra- structure and we have the potential to regenerate the local area.'

EARLY DAYS, QUICK WINS

A number of the leaders we spoke to stress the importance of notching up 'quick wins' in the early days of a change management programme. Heather Rabbatts says that visible wins, or 'getting some runs on the board', as she says, to use a sporting analogy, were a vital element in persuading the employees at the Borough of Lambeth that change was possible. 'I spent the first couple of months in the job talking to all sorts of people, from tenants to the political leadership, to try and get an idea of what was going on from the ground up. I asked all of them that if I said they could have three things from Lambeth, what they would be. I knew they would all have about 100, but they could have three. And while there wasn't a consensus on those three, it gave me enough to form a judgement about what we would do in the first year.'

One of the recurring complaints about Lambeth was the poor quality of its housing repairs system, one symptom of which was that the lighting on its housing estates was inadequate, with many broken bulbs that were never fixed. Rabbatts saw the opportunity to deliver a visible and tangible change:

'We probably broke every procurement rule in the book but one man and 60,000 light bulbs later, we got the lights working on our estates by Christmas, and that bought us enough time to fix what was a hugely complicated problem around housing repairs. You have to have visible changes that people can get hold of, particularly when you are running an organization that deals with the stuff of life. People are not interested in fancy strategies; they want lights that work. If you put enough of those in place, you win some credit to get some of the longer-term changes in place.

'When I took over, almost a third of the schools in Lambeth were classified as failing schools and we were about to have our educational responsibilities taken away from us, with good reason I think. You can't change those schools overnight but by the end of five years, none of our schools were failing. It's about getting the balance right, having sufficient critical presence of change so people think that maybe it can be done, which allows you to put in place the longer-running changes that ultimately put the organization on a better footing.'

Other leaders have used the same technique in order to persuade their people that change was possible and illustrate that it could happen quickly. Greg Dyke says that when he was appointed director-general of the BBC he spent several weeks visiting all of the regional offices in the country. 'I asked everyone I met the same two questions: what can I do to improve your life? And what can we do to improve the service to the viewer or listener? A lot of the answers were around just tiny things and so in the first couple of months I did as many of them as I could, partly to show that I was listening and partly to get them onside. For instance, the BBC had an internal costing system at the time that meant that if you wanted to borrow a CD out of the BBC's library it would cost you £15, when you could buy the same CD at HMV for £11. I got rid of that straightaway.'

Dyke also realized from visiting many of the regional radio stations run by the BBC that too many were operating on out-of-date technology. 'There was a capital investment programme to digitalize all of the local radio stations but it would have taken six or seven years to complete and in the meantime people were working with equipment that would have been out of date on an average media studies course. So I thought, hang on, we are a spending organization so why not spend the money over two years rather than six? As long as we spend the same amount the increased overall cost is small. So we did.'

When Dyke replaced John Birt as director-general of the BBC he inherited an organization that, while successful, was operating under a culture that many of its people felt stifled its creativity. Dyke took the view that creativity could be unleashed if some of the bureaucratic restraints within the organization were removed. 'It was clear from talking to the people at the coalface,' he says, 'they felt that whatever they achieved, they achieved in spite of the management. I tried to make them see that we were all trying to do the same thing.'

In common with Heather Rabbatts, Dyke found that quick and visible 'wins' were important in getting the message across that culture change was firmly on the agenda. The chance came when he saw one of the BBC's main buildings in White City:

'The building was a horrible, ugly, off-the-shelf design and only about 15 years old. The only nice thing about it was the atrium in the middle, but no-one was allowed into it. I asked why no-one could go in there and was told that you could go in, but you had to wear a hard hat if you did. But no-one could tell me why, although the magic words "health and safety" kept coming up. So I started chasing it and eventually the answer came back that we were not allowed in because there was no wheelchair ramp and it needed another exit door.

'I immediately decided that this was a good example and I would change it. Of course it cost more than it would have anywhere else but we spent about £100,000 and sorted it out. It turned into a lovely place and we put barbeques out there and a bar in the summer and opened it up for staff saying, this is yours now. I threw a party in there on the first night it opened and on that evening someone came up to me and said, does this mean we can go out on the balconies now? And someone else came up to me and said, does this mean my office doesn't have to be painted grey? So I found someone from the property department and said look, this is really working, they want to go out on the balconies! And he said, look what you've started now ...

'The point was that there are always rules in organizations that have been laid down but no-one remembers why. People just learn to live with them. The White City building became symbolic. I wrote a piece about it in the BBC's internal magazine and said, how many other examples like this are there out there? How many things have you been told that you can't do? What I did was tell them that it could be changed.'

The White City building idea gathered momentum in the organization and soon led to a range of initiatives – some of them, by Dyke's own admission, gimmicky – that were designed to spread the message that the days of bureaucracy at the BBC were over. One of them was 'cut the crap' cards, yellow football referee-style cards that were distributed to staff and which they could hold up at meetings if they felt that the discussion was too bureaucratic. 'It was about telling staff that they could challenge this stuff, they didn't have to live with it,' says Dyke. 'The culture change programme was all about telling them that they had the power, they could get on with things, that anyone in the organization could have ideas. In other words we took the elitism out of the organization, and it was incredibly effective.'

Dyke himself is one of the clearest examples of an empathetic leader – one that is able to inspire loyalty and affection among his employees. In the following section we will look more closely at authentic and empathetic approaches to leadership and how leaders in general interact with their followers.

WHAT LEADERS REALLY DO:

- Ensure their organization is prepared for change
- Create the conditions and atmosphere for change
- Have a feel for the 'art of the possible'
- Persuade people that change is both possible and desirable
- Own the change programme and never delegate responsibility for it
- Identify a clear message in communicating change and repeat it as often as necessary
- Minimize outside interference
- Put the people in place who will drive change from within
- Involve employees in decisions where appropriate
- Identify quick, visible 'wins' that gain goodwill for longer term change.

---

[1] *What Leaders Really Do,* Harvard Business Review, December 2001

PART THREE

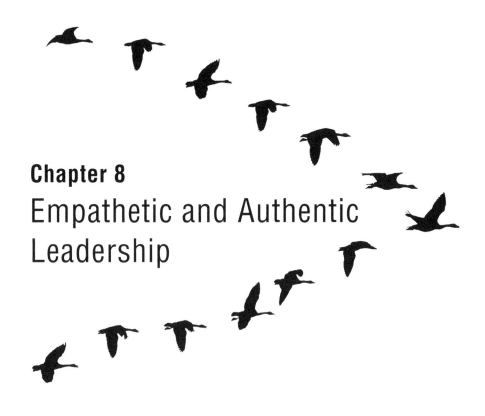

Chapter 8
Empathetic and Authentic Leadership

You achieve success as a leader when people will follow you any-where, if only out of curiosity.

General Colin Powell

In their book, *Why Should Anyone Be Led By You?* Rob Goffee and Gareth Jones argue that inspirational leaders are 'authentic chameleons', who manage relationships by knowing when to be close – empathizing with people and encouraging loyalty – and when to be distant in order to keep people focused on the goals. 'Crucially,' they say, 'leaders are able to create this distance without resorting to formal hierarchy.'

This balance between inspiring loyalty and even affection among followers while simultaneously preserving enough professional distance to command the necessary respect and authority, is a challenge for modern leaders. The underlying question, of course, is whether popularity and success as a leader are mutually exclusive. The advent of leaders such as Richard Branson of Virgin, who manage to engender high levels of loyalty and affection in their employees, suggests that the two can co-exist.

In recent years, the traditional leadership model of command and control has been replaced largely by transformational, empathetic and authentic leadership. Goffee and Jones argue that in these 'empowered' times, followers are hard to find, 'except by leaders who excel at capturing people's hearts, minds and spirits'.[1] They argue that in order to excel in these areas, a leader needs not only vision, energy, authority and strategic direction, but four additional qualities:

- They show that they are human and selectively reveal their weaknesses;
- They are adept at collecting and interpreting subtle interpersonal messages and as a result can intuitively sense mood within their organization;
- They manage employees with empathy, while giving them only what they need to achieve their best, rather than what they desire; and
- They dare to be different and capitalize on their uniqueness.

While a number of the leaders we spoke to clearly fall into Goffee and Jones' category of inspirational leaders who excel in capturing people's hearts and minds – Greg Dyke, Kevin Roberts and Patrick Cordingley being prime examples – it is clear that elements of the inspirational approach are apparent in the approach of every leader in our list, irrespective of their field. All of the leaders we spoke to believe strongly in an empathetic form of leadership, although few had consciously characterized their style as such. Most simply believe that it is the most effective approach, even those who lead the more traditional and strongly hierarchical organizations, such as the armed forces.

Sue Campbell of UK Sport says that she learned the value of engaging with people on her first day as a trainee physical education teacher, at a school in Manchester. 'My first class didn't even show up and I found them in the toilets, smoking,' she says. 'That was the day I realized that teaching is about people and not about the subject. If you can't get people to engage with you, the game is over. I learned very early on that a carrot works better than a stick. To me, leadership is the ability to take people not necessarily where they want to go, but where they can see the benefit is. And the skill lies in helping them understand that.'

EMPATHETIC LEADERSHIP

According to Charles Handy, in an average company you will find that 72% of employees are dissatisfied with their organization and 19% would actively sabotage it. A leader is nothing without followers and effective leaders understand that they need to work hard to get their staff onside if they are to achieve everything they want for their organization. 'You have to get them on your side because they can screw you, just by agreeing to do one thing and then doing another,' says Greg Dyke.

Dyke believes strongly in 'management without fear', something he has put into practice at every organization he has led. 'I always believe people work better if they enjoy it and feel valued. It amazes me how many organizations are run by scaring people and working them to death. I don't see the point. You don't have to treat people badly in order to get them to respond,' he says. 'In fact, it's quite the opposite.'

Dyke's approach converts in practice to a set of behaviour that is grounded in the belief that you should treat the people who work for you as you would treat your neighbour. While he was with London Weekend Television, Dyke started a tradition of throwing Christmas parties for employees' children. 'The goodwill you're buying when you have to do tough things is enormous. I can say, "I need your support".' Dyke also advocates allowing, wherever possible, people within an organization to make decisions that directly affect their everyday working lives. During his early days at the BBC, he says, he was told that a planned building in Leicester, which housed the radio station, was going to take two years longer than planned to complete:

> 'The current building was a terrible place. I discussed the options with the head of radio and the person in charge of the regions and then said, why don't we just let the staff decide? So we told them that they could either have this wonderful new building, which was going to take two years to complete, and stay in the current building until then or they could get out quickly and go somewhere else, but that would be nowhere near as nice as the new place. The staff voted for the new building, even though it meant waiting for two years. But from that moment on there was no moaning about it because it was their decision.'

At the BBC, Dyke encouraged a non-hierarchical approach to his leadership and worked hard to build a relationship with staff. 'I made sure everyone called me Greg. If anyone wrote to me, I replied. When I was at LWT I sent flowers to any member of staff when they had a child, but the BBC was simply too big to do that,' he explains. 'If someone was having a difficult time, I wrote them a note. If as a boss you communicate with people in times of tragedy and in times of joy, it makes a massive difference. It is absolutely essential and it is what decent human beings do anyway.'

Martin Glenn has taken a similar approach during his career as a CEO and says he was 'deliberately non-hierarchical' and favoured casual dress for workers and open plan offices. He actively encourages people to thank their co-workers because 'one of the big sappers of organizational energy is middle management failing to say thank you'. Overall, he believes in treating everyone in the organization as though they deserve consideration and merit:

> 'When I first went to Pepsico I found that the catering department, which was run by a subcontractor, was not invited to our Christmas party. The people who made my toast every morning weren't

invited. So of course we invited them. It's the universal idea of treating others as you would like to be treated yourself. It is tough being a CEO. It's more lonely and complicated than other roles but that doesn't excuse an inhuman – maybe that's too harsh – an impersonal type of behaviour.'

Sue Campbell adds that one of the most important elements of leadership is the 'old-fashioned notion' of values and trust. 'I want people who work with me to feel that they can absolutely trust me. I think that's a huge part of being a leader. If they don't trust me they are not going to follow me. People have to trust when you say, "I'm going left", that you are going to go left.'

'One of the crucial aspects of being able to motivate people is to have a sense of empathy,' agrees Heather Rabbatts. 'So when you say, "We're going to go over that hill", you elicit the response, "OK, we'll go over it with you".' Rabbatts believes she is fortunate in that she has the natural ability to engage with people from all backgrounds and at all levels. 'I can talk to the fans, to my manager, the players, to members of the board,' she says. 'I don't have any difficulty making connections with people and I took that totally for granted. But when I step back and reflect I think it is a very important element because it gives me an insight into what is going on in their lives. When you are trying to recalibrate an organization or give it a new vision, you have to bring a group of people with you who are also driven by hopes, dreams and insecurities. Unless you have some understanding of that, it's very difficult to drive a complex organization towards some shared objective.'

Kevin Roberts, worldwide CEO of Saatchi & Saatchi, believes that empathetic leadership is something that female leaders, in particular, excel in. 'My first three bosses were women and that defined my leadership style irrevocably from then on,' he says. 'Women taught me all about emotion, intuition, connectivity and empathy and I have found those to be core to leading people. I learned from my female bosses that nurturing and truly caring, not in a philanthropic way but in a demanding way, like the best families, is very effective.'

CARING LEADERSHIP

The leaders we spoke to universally agree that the 'command and control' approach to leadership is defunct and that an empathetic and caring approach will inevitably get the best out of people. It is hardly surprising, then, that these same leaders make a concerted effort to know the people who work for them, and closely monitor mood within their organization.

The military leaders feel particularly strongly that knowing their men is a vitally important element of good leadership. Lord Inge explains that military leaders have an 'all-embracing responsibility' for their men that does not have an equivalent in the business world, but adds that any leader that takes the trouble to know and understand the people who are working for them will inevitably get more out of them. Major General Patrick Cordingley adds that knowing the capabilities of the men you are commanding is vital to successful military leadership: 'Everyone will have a strength or weakness and you are not going to get the best out of people unless you play to those strengths and recognize the weaknesses. So it is logical that you should train with the people you are going to fight alongside.'

Lord Inge tells of an important lesson he learned from his company sergeant major during his first posting as a young officer in Hong Kong:

> *'Every morning after the parade he would ask me about one of my soldiers and I knew that I was not answering the question properly. Eventually I asked him why he was asking and he said, "I have been watching you, sir, and you look at their boots, their belts, their rifles and their cap badges, but you don't look them in the eye. The most important thing you will do is get to know those 33 sets of eyes because they will tell you if the men are frightened, whether they are drinking too much, or have been bullied, or if something has upset them." I said that was wonderful advice and asked why he hadn't told me that before. And he said "Because if I told you from the word go, you would have forgotten. Now you'll never forget."'*

Colonel Bob Stewart says he learned a similar lesson from his company commander early on in his military career: 'I remember going to him once to complain that I was sitting around in barracks doing administration and it was a bloody waste of time and I had many better things to do. So he said to me, "Do you know every man in your platoon?" and I said, yes, of course I did. And he said, "Do you know the names of their mothers, fathers, brothers, sisters and girlfriends?" Of course I did not. So he told me to go away and learn them. That shut me up. There's nothing more impressive than knowing your soldiers and really caring about them.' Colonel Stewart remembers an occasion where he saw this theory put into practice:

'Major General Cathcart, the Queen's cousin, was the general officer commanding while I was in Berlin. I had met him a couple of times and he was so far above us in rank it was almost impossible to contemplate. One day I saw him coming towards me so I came to attention, saluted and said, good morning, sir. He looked at me and said, "Good morning, Bob". I thought it was incredible that he knew my name. Then I watched him go further down the corridor and saw him kneel down beside the cleaner who was washing the floor and he asked her in German how her husband was, because he had heard that he had been ill. He had a huge influence on how I did my job later on.'

The next question for leaders is how to communicate what could be seen as a rather esoteric approach through the organization. 'How do you reinforce a company's values?' asks Sue Campbell. 'How do you reinforce that you really do care about people? I could stay longer and work harder and that would be easy, but it's important to do it the right way, by caring for your colleagues and making an effort for others. You have to find ways of making people feel that they matter, otherwise the values of an organization just become something you talk about, rather than something you live.'

Some of the leaders make the point that it is important not only to care about employees and workers, but to show clearly that you care. Colonel Bob Stewart says that when it comes to the management of people, even in the military, good leaders will 'clearly and convincingly put them first'. He relates how he adopted this approach himself while he was on duty in Bosnia and Herzegovina:

> *'We came to Vitez, where we would have our base. My first priority was to find a building, a cafeteria or a restaurant, where the soldiers could relax off-duty. After we had done that, we found somewhere that could be used as the sergeants' mess and then lastly, three months later, I eventually found somewhere that could be used as an officers' mess. You need to show clear, convincing proof of where your priority lies, through your own actions.'*

Empathetic leaders also recognize and understand when one of their team is facing difficulties. Sharkey Ward tells of an episode during the Falklands conflict, which came shortly after a pilot in another squadron had suffered post-traumatic stress after shooting down an Argentinian fighter jet and was eventually sent home amid inaccurate suggestions that he lacked moral fibre:

> *'One of my pilots lost a plane overboard while preparing for take-off during a heavy storm – thank God he ejected in time – and it completely destroyed him. It was the second time he had had to eject from an aircraft and now he couldn't go near the flight deck or into the crew room without physically shaking. I discussed it with the doctor, who was a good friend of mine. I asked the doctor to examine him, to find that he had a problem with his back and to send him home. Later I called [the pilot] in to see me and told him he had done a great job and we were really proud of him. I said I was sorry that he had gone over the side and got wet and said the doctor had told me that he had a bad back and he had no choice, I was sending him home. I could see how relieved he was.'*

SENSING MOOD

It is undoubtedly easier for leaders in smaller organizations to sense the mood within the organization. For leaders of larger organization, the challenge is greater, particularly when faced with the time pressures of their own role. Sebastian Coe is well aware of this dilemma, as the Organising Committee for the London Olympic Games and Paralympic Games is growing at an exponential rate:

> *'When there were just 60 people here I knew what was going on. I knew that someone working in the communications department had a son who was in hospital. But we are going to double our numbers every year between now and 2012 and in the final year we will have around 3000 people here. At every team meeting at the moment we are greeting 10 or 12 new people. I think it's very important as the team gets bigger to hang on to what's going on. It was much easier when there were 60 people than it is now there are over 130.'*

The captains of sporting teams work and train alongside their team mates and so generally have a keen sense of when something is wrong. 'You just have a gut feeling when the team is up or down,' says Nasser Hussain. 'The team bus is generally a good time to have a look. I used to keep an eye on the players, where they were sitting, have they got their Walkmans on, are they preparing for the game, do they need a quiet moment. I was never concerned about mood swings, though, because I had them myself.' The rugby captain Martin Johnson says he also grew accustomed to particular players' habits in the run-up to a game, so could recognize when they were acting outside of their normal routine or behaviour and perhaps something was wrong.

Leadership can be an isolating role, particularly in a large organization. As a result, leaders often have to work hard to ensure that they have enough contact with people to recognize when something is wrong, or engineer an atmosphere where workers feel happy to report to them freely. 'I've been in this job since 1992 so I have a good instinct about the place that's based on years of practical experience,' says Gail Rebuck of Random House. 'I usually gauge things just by chatting to people and listening.' Even so, she adds that it is not always easy for the leader to know when things are going wrong. 'It's getting better, but the challenge I do have is that often people will not tell me about problems until it's almost too late to help solve them.'

A number of leaders say that informal meetings, such as meal-times, are invaluable in allowing them to assess the mood within an organization and many, including Greg Dyke and Charles Dunstone, frequently eat in the staff canteen. Major General Patrick Cordingley says that he made sure that he ate with his men as often as possible:

> 'The commander needs to know what the men are thinking and it is relatively easy to gauge mood when you talk to someone over breakfast, for instance, and he has been on guard during the night. He might have been out in the desert, watching for the enemy and that can be quite unnerving. Your eyes start playing tricks on you or you start thinking, am I ever going to survive this? But at breakfast I could sit next to a soldier and say, what were you doing last night? And he would say he had been on guard and did I think it was going to be alright. And that was very useful because I had the opportunity to say directly to him that yes, of course it was.'

Dame Stella Rimington also understands the benefit of informal discussions with staff, something she learned during her early career as an archivist in Worcester County Record Office. Her respected but somewhat austere boss insisted that the team took regular tea breaks with him:

> 'He had a big teapot that was large enough to serve us all and he used to ring the bell when it was time for tea. I like the image of the big teapot – it creates a moment where people have to interact. It's like a meeting, only in less formal circumstances. It's possible that that comes from having a family and realizing that you get the best information out of them over meals, when you all sit around the table and talk about what has gone on during the day. You can see whether people are interacting or not.'

She recognizes, though, that in an organization as large and diverse as MI5, regular teabreaks with staff are not going to address the problem of communication. Instead, Dame Stella took the view that as long as the right communication tiers and culture were in place, the right information would reach the top. 'It's all very well going around and talking to people, but you have to have some kind of system for communicating upwards in an organization and that can only come through a proper structure,' she says. 'That means section meetings and a culture where people feel it is OK to say what they think. It's also about picking the right people to hold the positions lower down the organization.'

Sharkey Ward agrees that while he could often sense that a member of his squadron had a problem, 'it is far better if you have someone at grass roots level who will tell you if something is amiss. I made sure that no-one was afraid to come up to me in the bar and tell me what they thought'.

Sir Clive Woodward used a less formal reporting structure while coach of the England team and relied on the medical team to tell him if a player had a problem.

'I got a huge amount of feedback from the medical staff, both good and bad. The medical room is a very important place where a lot of discussions take place. It was also a room that I hardly ever went into. I always met with the medical staff separately because if there were coaches around there was a danger that the players would clam up. They trusted the medical staff and rightly so, because they would never break a confidence. But the doctor might come to me and say, why not give this player the day off tomorrow, I think he needs it.'

DELIVERING BAD NEWS

Redundancy, restructuring and streamlining all translate to the same thing for employees – bad personal news. Inevitably it falls to the leaders to manage these difficult situations but how do leaders reconcile an empathetic leadership style with laying off their own workers?

It is inevitable that any leader will have to face these difficult decisions at some point in their career. Some of the leaders we spoke to have faced large-scale redundancies in their own organization and have learned important lessons through their own experiences.

While chief executive of London Weekend Television, Greg Dyke reduced the number of employees from 1400 to 800. He makes the obvious point that morale among the remaining staff was not a problem 'because they were all still there' but adds that he learned from the LWT experience that announcing an intention to make large-scale redundancies is rarely a good idea. 'That's what I learned. If you announce that you are going to sack 15% of your workforce you destabilize everyone. Don't announce it, do it privately and then be generous.'

Both Dyke and Heather Rabbatts, who saw through large-scale redundancies at the Borough of Lambeth, stress that it is vital that the programme is owned by the leader and not outsourced to the HR department. 'You can't hand over management of the difficult things to someone else. Managers have to manage. HR can only advise,' says Dyke.

The leaders who have faced large-scale redundancies also say that they were careful to clearly explain the reason for the redundancies. 'At LWT I met with everybody in groups of about 40 and said that there was a licence auction coming up and only the most efficient organizations were going to win, so this was what we were going to do,' says Greg Dyke. 'I also said that we had cash at the moment, so we were going to be generous.'

Gail Rebuck took the same approach when announcing redundancies at Random House. She announced the plan to the entire organization, after which everyone immediately met with their manager to discuss their own personal situation. 'I wanted to be very generous with the people who did lose their jobs and we offered counselling,' she explains. 'We did it in as ethical a way as possible. And although it was a huge revolution there wasn't any acrimony because I think everyone looked at the evidence and thought well, I would do the same thing, even if it meant bad news for them personally.'

Rabbatts agrees that direct, honest and above all, timely communication is the only way forward when dealing with redundancies. 'You can't leave people thinking that they are going to be one of the pool of 1000 who will go. You have to do it quickly. The worst thing for everyone involved is apprehension so it's much better to confront people as soon as possible rather than wait until you have the perfect roadmap, by which point everyone is fuelled by anxiety. How you do it is also important. If you treat people properly and with dignity and understand how difficult it is, that helps to maintain a sense of morale within the organization.'

Rabbatts also kept up a consistent communication of her vision for the Borough, particularly when negotiating with the various unions that were representing the workers:

'During my first 18 months with Lambeth I used to meet with the unions every fortnight. I took the view that it was all about clarity. I would negotiate on terms and conditions, but I would not negotiate on the vision. By the end I think even the white collar trade unions recognized that we had to deal with the issues, like the massive problem with sickness absences, for the sake of the members who were turning up for work every day. We restored what I thought was an appropriate balance between proper trade union recognition and managerial leadership.'

While a caring and empathetic leadership style clearly works for these leaders, it is not necessarily something that can be imitated. Empathetic leaders tend to be empathetic people who have adapted to the leadership role. In the following section we will look more closely at this model of authentic leadership put forward by Rob Goffee and Gareth Jones in *Why Should Anyone Be Led By You?*

WHAT EMPATHETIC LEADERS DO:

- Treat everyone in the organization as deserving consideration and merit
- Involve people in decisions that directly affect them wherever possible
- Persuade, rather than push
- Avoid hierarchies
- Make efforts to know their people
- Demonstrate that they care and illustrate clearly where their priorities lie
- Interact informally with staff
- Encourage open and informal channels of communication

AUTHENTIC LEADERSHIP

Goffee and Jones argue strongly that in order to be a leader, you must be yourself. 'Followers want to be led by a person, not a role holder or a position filler or a bureaucrat', they say. Goffee and Jones's central argument is that effective leaders know how to be themselves, with skill. In other words, they identify what makes them effective as a leader and play to those strengths.

Goffee and Jones argue that it is not possible to succeed as a leader unless you have some sense of who you are.[2] People want to be led by a person, not an automaton, and satisfying that need requires that a leader understands him or herself and their own strengths and weaknesses. 'Showing people who you are requires a degree of self-knowledge (or at least self-awareness) as well as self-disclosure', say Jones and Goffee.

The leaders we spoke to show a high degree of self-awareness and were more than willing to disclose and discuss where they thought their weaknesses lay. Nasser Hussain, for instance, says that his strengths lay in tactics and man management, even though he was not the best player in the team, and his weakness, towards the end, lay in his poor body language. Sue Campbell says that her weakness is impatience: 'I've had to work at that because I'm always in a hurry to get things done. I've had to learn to temper that because leadership is about taking people with you and you can only go, sometimes, at the speed of the slowest person.'

All of the leaders believe that recognizing and understanding their own character allowed them to be a more effective leader, partly because it allowed them to address their weaknesses themselves, and partly because it helped them in recruiting a close team who complemented their own skills and character. 'It's a very sensible thing to recognize where you are not very strong, and I tried to do that,' says Sharkey Ward. 'I knew I could be cheeky so I allowed my senior pilot to do a lot of the communicating on my behalf.'

Kevin Roberts, the worldwide CEO of Saatchi & Saatchi, freely admits that he was unsuited to one of his previous roles, as chief executive of the Lion Nathan brewing company in New Zealand:

'I wasn't great. I was there for seven years and it was a declining industry. It was all about closing down breweries, reducing costs and laying off people, all the things I'm crap at and don't believe in. I hated it and all the inspirational stuff I'm good at were of little avail in that situation. I didn't want to lay off people who were redundant through no fault of their own. Someone had to do it but frankly that someone wasn't me. I don't think leaders are that transportable.'

Some of the leaders have actively tried to improve on their weak areas. Colonel Bob Stewart says that he 'put a lot of work, personally' into his management style and deliberately changed his leadership style before he went to Bosnia. He took an analytical approach, dissecting the views others had of him as a leader (gleaned from feedback reports) and identifying the areas where he needed to change his behaviour. 'I took a format from officers' confidential reports and judged myself against the criteria of an officer,' he explains. 'The reports suggested that I was seen as too laid-back, too friendly and too verbose. One said that "if anything, he has a slight tendency to wear his heart on his sleeve, for which he is clearly much respected, even revered, within the battalion". That's an adverse comment. So I wrote down my own private thoughts about my problem areas, my leadership style and the things I had to work on. I needed to watch verbosity. I needed to be mentally tougher when casualties were imposed and I needed to be more practical.'

Even so, leaders must invariably act as leaders. The leaders we spoke to agree that they are authentic, in the sense that their leadership style is dictated by their personality, strengths and weaknesses. Many, though, recognize that there is an element of performance in their role as leader. As Martin Glenn puts it:

'You need huge self-discipline to do this job, particularly in the way you come across to people. If I was always myself and always showed what I am feeling, I think that would be a slight failure on my part. I don't think people want to know if their leader is facing inner demons. There have been occasions where I have said to a broader management group that I am struggling with an issue and I'm happy to say that I don't know the answer to something. But I think you need to keep your personal crises to yourself because there is a degree of image that people want to see. You have a professional face to put on.'

Heather Rabbatts agrees: 'There are of course times when you are tired and don't want to be the high-energy person, but you have to be. And there are times when I really want to lose my temper, but I never, ever have. I had a terrible temper as a child but I have absolutely learned to control it. I will shut the door and scream but I will rarely raise my voice to someone, even though sometimes I may dearly wish to.'

Nasser Hussain, the former England cricket captain, is among the leaders who argue that followers will see through inauthentic leaders in a second. 'The general rule of thumb for me was always to be myself because the players are very clever and the moment you strike a false note, they will see through you. That said, though, at times I did have to appear more cross than I really was.' Nasser believes that he was a better captain because the players saw and recognized his weaknesses. 'I was only averaging 37 runs an innings and I threw my toys out of the cot when I was [bowled] out from time to time. The team saw me as human and I think that made me a better skipper. Graham Gooch and Alec Stewart [the previous captains] were so perfect that it was difficult to live up to that.'

Dame Stella Rimington doubts that she would have been able to play a role while director-general of MI5, even if she wanted to. 'I was myself and that seemed the right approach. I would rather withdraw than play a role,' she says. 'I'm the type of person where what you see is what you get and if that didn't work in any given situation, I might try to manipulate things. But I think that on the whole [being yourself] does work because people tend to respond to that.' Charles Dunstone of the Carphone Warehouse agrees: 'You might do something that doesn't work out perfectly but at least it's you. The integrity and the honesty of the fact that you are being you is what matters. It's almost as though your frailty matters when you are a leader because people can see that there is an inherent truth in what you do.'

Even so, in some situations, particularly organizations with a well-established and inflexible hierarchy, being yourself can be a risky proposition. Sharkey Ward, who commanded a squadron of Sea Harriers during the Falklands War, says that from his very first days as squadron commander he decided that he would do things his own way, and not the Navy way:

'That caused quite a stir at [the squadron's Naval Air Station] Yeovilton. All of the other squadron commanders would stay after hours in case the base commander wanted to speak to them late in the evening. I announced straight away that I was going to leave at 5.30p.m. every day, that all of my pilots should do the same, and if anyone wanted to talk to me, they could talk to me the next morning. No-one could understand it. My senior officer thought I was an idiot. But my squadron proved to be the most operationally efficient in the Fleet Air Arm.'

THE STORIES PEOPLE TELL

Leaders are constantly under the spotlight, even when they do not realize that they are. 'You don't realize when you are boss how every little thing you do is judged,' says Greg Dyke. 'People notice the tiniest things.' Dyke argues that a leader's success is measured by how they are viewed by employees and others that they meet. In the same way that an organization's reputation depends to a large extent on the way its employees talk about it in their everyday lives, what says most about a leader, says Dyke, is the stories that people tell.

'I am chancellor of a university and was presenting at a degree ceremony recently,' says Dyke. 'For the people there, it is a really important day. I met the father of twin girls who had taken part and he said, they really liked you, one because you smiled and the other because you told her that you liked her shoes. Management is about those small stories.' He also tells of a conversation he had with his BBC driver, who was taking him from appointment to appointment. The two men were talking one day and Dyke asked him about his holiday plans. The driver told him that his family's holiday plans had recently fallen through because of an administrative mistake by a holiday company. Dyke immediately offered him use of his own holiday home. Within hours, says Dyke, the story had spread around the BBC.

Dyke is not alone in understanding the power of small stories. He relates a conversation he had with Mo Mowlem, the late MP:

> 'Mo Mowlem told me that when she visited anywhere as Secretary of State for Northern Ireland she would go up to the receptionist first and say, hello, I'm Mo Mowlem, who are you? And later, she'd write down the name. The next time she went to the same place she would go to reception and say hello, I'm Mo and the receptionist would say hello, I'm Joan. So Mo would say, isn't Muriel on today? Those things matter. In the end it's about the stories people tell about you.'

While Dyke believes strongly that you get the best out of employees by nurturing, supporting and treating them well, he says that he was also aware that his public image was important and was not beyond making a grand gesture if he thought it would help in the long term. 'I suppose it could be quite calculated at times, what I did, but your people have to know that you put them first.' He explains how, during his tenure as director-general of the BBC, there was a serious fire at his home one night as he was on his way back from the Conservative Party Conference: 'I was due to speak at a big BBC conference the next day and I got a message to say that they had announced that I wasn't coming because of the fire. I said that I would be there as soon as I could and I turned up looking a mess, but I spoke at the conference. The people there would have gone back to their offices and said, "Guess what? He turned up even though his house has burned down!" It told people that they mattered.'

Heather Rabbatts recognizes that she had a point to make when appointed vice-chair of Millwall football club, particularly with the fans. She says it was vitally important to go out and talk to people as much as possible, especially the fans. 'It can be disarming,' she says. 'They may not want to like you and I don't necessarily want them to, I just want them to respect what it is we're trying to do.' Rabbatts chose to attend the club's forums where fans are invited to meet the club's management and ask questions:

'After one of the meetings this guy came up to me and he looked like, well, a classic National Front candidate. He said to me "So, have you got anything against the white working class?" and I said no, I hadn't, that my father was a Peckham boy and his mother used to clean people's doorsteps for a living. I also said that my dad had had the very good sense to marry a Jamaican woman and asked if he had a problem with that. He said no, he didn't. The following day someone said to me that there was a posting from the same guy on the Millwall fans website and he had written that he wasn't expecting to like me but he thought I was alright. So we'll see.'

Military leaders also recognize that reputation and visibility are vital in leadership, particularly when they are leading a large group of people and especially in a conflict situation. 'Leadership doesn't necessarily have to be from the front,' says Colonel Bob Stewart, 'but it has to be in front in the people's mind. They have to understand that you are with them.' Major General Patrick Cordingley agrees and says that he would make visible gestures to back up that point while in the Gulf: 'I made absolutely certain that the men knew that if, for instance, they were having an inoculation against anthrax or bubonic plague, I would go and have my injection with them.'

Colonel Stewart says that while he was in Bosnia helping to negotiate a ceasefire, he unwittingly overheard two of his men talking:

'I was utterly and completely exhausted. I can't remember sleeping much. I was getting up at 6am in order to escort the various warlords to the conference across the lines, and we were getting shot at and attacked, then we'd run the conference for seven or eight hours and then take them back, getting back to our base at two in the morning.

'Anyway, I had a short break at one point and was sitting on an ammunition crate in a dark corridor with my sergeant major, having a mug of tea. There were no lights because the town was under fire and the electricity had gone. Two of my squaddies appeared at the other end of the corridor, and lit up cigarettes. They didn't know we were there. One of them said "I've been here two days and I've never seen the commanding officer." The other one said, "You've not seen Colonel Bob? Have you been on the field yet?" The first said no, he hadn't, and the other said, "Well, when you are in the field and under fire for the first time, look in front of you and you will see Colonel Bob." From that point I was no longer tired. I was floating.'

VISIBILITY

Leaders, particularly those in a large organization, understand that it is important to be visible and accessible – within reason – to as many employees as possible. Greg Dyke was particularly effective at this while at the BBC, using a combination of meetings, visits and email communication to ensure that as many of the organization's employees as possible *felt* that they knew him, even if they saw him comparatively rarely. Heather Rabbatts says she shared Dyke's approach:

> *'It is very unusual, particularly in a huge organization like the BBC or the Borough of Lambeth, which had 10,000 people, to have that sort of impact and make a connection with people. It's easy to get driven back to the desk and office. And Greg absolutely did not do that. Wherever I have worked I have never locked the door or hidden behind a desk. I have always gone out and about. It got harder and harder in the last few years at Lambeth to stay visible, such were the pressures of what we were trying to do. I seemed to be in a sea of meetings from morning to night. Walkabouts tend to be the first thing to get crowded out. So I tried to hang on to them.'*

The leaders we spoke to who had joined an existing and established organization all stressed the importance of personal site visits in developing their understanding of the business. Greg Dyke and Heather Rabbatts both spent a number of months visiting the various areas of their respective organizations in the very early days of their leadership.

Dyke says that during the first few weeks of his appointment, he visited as many of the regional BBC sites as possible, some of which had not seen a VIP visit for years. He always made sure that he had proper access to staff, which allowed him to assess what was really happening at the grass roots level. 'When I went visiting anywhere I wouldn't let them put on a private lunch, ever,' he says. 'We ate with the staff and asked specifically that staff from as many areas as possible be there at the same time.'

Charles Dunstone also believes in the importance of being visible and accessible as a leader and it is something he has tried to maintain as Carphone Warehouse has grown. In common with many of the leaders we spoke to, his office has glass walls or a permanently open door. 'I think it's important to be in an office that's accessible and to eat in the canteen with everyone else,' he says. 'You don't want to patronize people, but just try to be as much a normal member of the team as you can.'

Maintaining a visible presence is particularly important for military leaders, especially in times of conflict. Major General Patrick Cordingley commanded over 5000 men during the first Gulf War and says that he always took the time to talk to as many of his men as possible. 'I know they liked seeing me and I always enjoyed seeing them as a result. There were techniques that I used. For instance, a lot of the soldiers played chess while we were out there, so if I went into an area where I didn't know the men particularly well and I saw someone playing chess, I would go and play with them. It was a bit of a waste of time, strictly speaking, because it might take half an hour but if they beat me – and they often would – they would love being able to tell everyone that they had beaten the brigade commander. Those sorts of things really helped and I think it is an important thing to do, although it wasn't studied on my part.'

He adds, though, that occasionally he was forced to be more visible than he might otherwise have chosen. While stationed in the Saudi Arabian desert with his troops and preparing to move into Kuwait, Major General Cordingley lived alongside his tank crew and the rest of the brigade:

'We were on a barren, open plain for five months, living cheek by jowl amongst each other. It never got dramatically difficult but I can tell you that if you get up in the morning and do everything in front of everyone else, washing, shaving, going to the loo, well, it does get quite wearing.

'The thing about soldiers is that they know you are vulnerable without clothes. So they would wait until the shower truck arrived – which wasn't often, about every 10 days – before asking the tricky questions. We would line up and wait while four got under the water at a time. Of course it wasn't my natural habitat so they would ask questions while all of this was going on: "When's the war starting, sir?"'

Major General Cordingley adds that he was careful, because they were all living in such close proximity, not to spend too much time sitting amongst the men. 'They would probably find that inhibiting,' he says. The balance between being visible as a leader and becoming omnipresent within the organization is something that Gail Rebuck of Random House feels is important to consider. 'Leaders have to know when to be visible and when to be invisible,' she says. 'You don't want to be a crushing presence because people will think that you will not want to grow leaders internally. You have to give people room to grow and to become future leaders themselves while at the same time, when things are tough, show that you are there and are part of the team.'

KEEP YOUR DISTANCE

Jones and Goffee argue that leaders know when to be close to people and when to be distant. The leaders we spoke to recognized that it was potentially dangerous to become too close to the people you lead, and took steps to ensure that they maintained distant, while empathetic. Sir Clive Woodward, for instance, says that he has never celebrated socially with the players after a win, even when England won the rugby World Cup in 2003. 'You have to be careful,' he says bluntly, 'because you might have to fire someone one day.' Nasser Hussain describes his own approach as being 'part of the team but also apart from the team'.

That said, Sir Clive Woodward worked hard to build a relationship with the players and used to routinely invite them to his home, while making sure that a sense of professional distance was maintained. 'If

they are in your house you can talk to them properly and they tend to
open up a bit more,' he says. 'I said from the moment I took over the
England team, you all know where I live. You only have to ring and
you can come and see me, 24 hours a day. But I said I didn't expect
them to do that unless there was a real issue. In the seven years I
was in charge I think four players came to see me and none of them
wanted to talk about rugby. They all had personal issues or problems
they wanted to discuss, and we could do that because we had already
built those bridges.'

Heather Rabbatts says that leaders have to accept that they cannot
necessarily be popular and an effective leader. 'There are always
going to be moments when you have to make some really tough decisions and maybe fire someone and you can't confuse the issue,' she
says. She adds that while she might go for a drink after work with colleagues, she would never invite a manager to her home or go to theirs
on a social basis, unless it was within a much wider group. 'You can't
be friends, you can't move into that level of intimacy. Some people
that I no longer work with have since become good friends but at the
time, there has to be a boundary.'

In the following chapters we look more closely at how leader motivate, encourage and work alongside their employees.

WHAT AUTHENTIC LEADERS DO:

- Have a high degree of self-awareness
- Understand their strengths and weaknesses and adapt their
  leadership approach accordingly
- Recognize that there is an element of performance in leadership
- Are visible and accessible
- Avoid setting themselves apart from employees
- Keep a professional distance.

---

[1] *Why Should Anyone Be Led By You*, Harvard Business Review, p 63
[2] *Why Should Anyone Be Led By You?* p 29

Chapter 9
Motivation, Inspiration and Morale

Leadership is the art of getting someone else to do something you want done because he wants to do it.

Dwight D Eisenhower

While a leader may be tactically brilliant and make inspired decisions, his or her skills will have little impact unless the followers buy in completely to the message. Working out how to best motivate employees and sustain that motivation over the long term, is one of the major challenges for leaders. John Kotter argues that the key to keeping people moving in the right direction, and ensuring that they have the energy to overcome any barriers in their way, is to appeal to basic but often untapped human needs, values and emotions.[1] 'Motivation and inspiration energize people, not by pushing them in the right direction as control mechanisms do but by satisfying basic human needs for achievement, recognition, self-esteem, a feeling of control over one's life, and the ability to live up to one's ideals,' says Kotter. 'Such feelings touch us deeply and elicit a powerful response.'

Professor Brian Morgan, director of the Creative Leadership and Enterprise Centre at University of Wales, argues that the issue of motivation is an area that clearly highlights the difference between transactional and transformational leaders. 'Transactional leaders motivate people in the direction of the established goals by clarifying roles and tasks and providing rewards if employees perform in excess of their contractual obligations,' he says. 'But they also avoid giving new or additional direction if the old methods are working. If performance goals are being met they tend to focus on tactical issues and work within the current systems.'

Transformational leaders, by contrast, emphasis vision, values and strategic issues and get things done by motivating others to think differently about the organization: 'They take calculated risks to challenge and change existing structures and they succeed by aligning internal structures to reinforce and achieve the overarching goals.' These leaders tend to be described as creative, innovative or inspirational.

Whatever their approach, the leaders we spoke to agree that motivation underpins successful leadership. Ron Dennis of McLaren says that 'motivation is critical to success in leadership. Once you have taken a decision, communicating it and creating the necessary motivation is very important. If you haven't got a motivated group of people with you then your chances of success are much slimmer. But motivation can be difficult to achieve, particularly in adversity.'

Martin Glenn, however, argues that it is more difficult to create a sense of urgency in a team that is winning than it is in a team that is losing. (Martin Johnson agrees with this view, saying that it was often harder as a team to keep the motivation going throughout a game when they were winning. 'Sometimes it's nice to be behind at half time because it gives everyone a gee-up,' he says.) 'Terry Leahy [the CEO of Tesco] talks about that problem all of the time,' says Glenn.

'What you have to do is, when you get to the top of the tree, define the forest as the next target. It's always about giving people targets.'

In reality, motivation within an organization is closely linked to a number of factors, many of which will be covered in more detail in the following chapters. It is accepted that employees are generally motivated if:

- They believe in the vision, direction or objectives (however it is labelled) of the organization and its leader;
- They feel they are trusted and have been well informed;
- They have been presented with challenging but achievable goals; and
- They feel that their organization cares for their welfare.

Our leaders run a wide variety of organizations in different fields, the circumstances of which will directly impact on the motivational aspects of their leadership. All of the leaders, however, actively attempted to create an atmosphere where their employees or team felt valued, nurtured and trusted.

For some, motivation has more specific requirements. Sue Campbell, who runs UK Sport, is among the leaders who believe that motivation is closely tied to the working atmosphere of an organization. Happy workers are productive workers, in other words. For Campbell, that means an atmosphere where people enjoy working and are energized in a positive and productive way. 'To me,' she says, 'work should be a place to have fun. I don't mean that it's frivolous, but I want to hear laughter in the place. I want to hear good arguments going on around me. I want to feel energy in the place.'

Sir Clive Woodward makes the point that few leaders can afford to take their eye off the ball when it comes to motivation:

'It's very easy to demotivate people. You can destroy something with the stroke of a pen by doing something really stupid, or saying something stupid. You can spend years building something up and then destroy it overnight, by allowing one player in the team who

shouldn't be there, for example. Demotivation is very easy. Moti-
vating, keeping it going, is very tough. That's leadership.'

That said, leaders from the sporting world (and sometimes, from the
military) argue that motivation is a natural part of the package of a
successful team. Martin Johnson, captain of the World Cup-winning
English rugby team, says that if he ever had to talk about the work
ethic or determination with his team, he would have already been in
serious in trouble. The players had to be seriously motivated in order
to be selected for the team in the first place and were well aware that
there were many other capable players biting at their heels if they
failed to deliver. Motivation was rarely a problem.

Sharkey Ward makes a similar point about 801 Naval Air Squadron, which he commanded during the Falklands conflict. Ward had
been closely involved with the Sea Harrier aircraft since it first
entered service barely three years before the war (he calls the aircraft his 'protégé') and was evangelical about its capabilities. This
was reflected within the squadron team, who were all equally enthu-
siastic about the aircraft:

> *'It's difficult to explain but when you have a squadron like that and
> a new aircraft, it's recognized as the cream of the Fleet Air Arm.
> Everyone wants to be part of it and everyone wants to make it work.
> Motivation was not a problem.*

> *'My team were totally motivated and absolutely wonderful. When
> you have an unmotivated team usually you have an unhappy team
> and an unhappy team in the services when you're away from home
> for months on end usually leads to a string of misdemeanours,
> defaulters as we call them in the Navy. People break the rules, get
> into fights or whatever. For the total time I was with my squadron,
> we had two minor defaulters in the whole time, which was quite
> amazing.'*

Ward's overwhelming enthusiasm for the Sea Harrier and absolute
loyalty towards the men in his squadron, though, undoubtedly served

to create and feed the group's motivation. Ian Mortimer, who was a flight lieutenant in Ward's squadron, says that the men 'went everywhere on the crest of a wave with Sharkey. He is a dynamo. He knows exactly what he wants and how he's going to do it. And he always goes at it flat out.'

Not everyone, though, is in the fortunate position of leading a team of people that are already motivated by the situation in which they find themselves. Major General Patrick Cordingley relates the difficulty he faced in maintaining the morale and motivation of his troops in the run-up to the liberation of Kuwait in 1991. By the time the order came for them to move forward, many of the men had been stationed in the Saudi Arabian desert for more than 20 weeks:

'One of the problems we had emerged after we had been there for a couple of months. Initially we did a lot of training with the 15,000 men we had in the middle of the desert. We'd done a lot of training with them especially to check that all the guns were firing in the right direction, but what then? I had thousands of men all wondering what to do next. We realized really quite quickly that we had to keep them occupied, so we exercised them as much as possible. But that in itself was difficult because if you did too much you would run out of ammunition, or break an engine ...'

Nasser Hussain, the former captain of the England cricket team, makes the point that different personalities will require different motivational techniques. He cites the example of two players in his team who had sharply contrasting personalities:

'Darren Gough loves the big stage and loves the cameras. His fear of failure is very low and he has an enormous will to get the job done. At the other end of the scale I had Andy Caddick, who is six foot tall, has swing and ability and should be the best player of all time but he wakes up nervous before every game and has a huge fear of failure.

'So if I had them both bowling at once I'd tell Gough that the guy at the other end was struggling and I needed him to pull us through. He'd take the ball and say, let me get on with it. To Caddick, I'd say not to worry about getting wickets because the pitch had nothing in it. The opposition would probably bat until lunch and I'd be happy if he got one wicket. He would think that the pressure was off, and relaxed. It's not rocket science. It's just about knowing the individual.'

CELEBRATING SUCCESSES

John Kotter argues that supporting employees in their efforts is an important element in motivating them to meet the overall vision of an organization. 'Good leaders recognize and reward success,' says Kotter, 'which not only gives people a sense of accomplishment but also makes them feel like they belong in an organization.'[2] Kevin Roberts says this is particularly important within Saatchi & Saatchi because many of his employees have not had enough recognition for their efforts in the past. 'Some come from broken homes, or from tough working class environments or have had trouble passing exams.'

Both Greg Dyke and Sue Campbell believe that celebrating success is an important element in sustaining motivation among a workforce. Dyke says that he learned the importance of celebrating successes, even small ones, within an organization while visiting a US company. 'They had a sizable room in this place that was set aside just to store presents,' he says. 'It was full of balloons and plants and little things that anyone in the company could choose to send to a colleague if they had helped them with something and they thought they deserved a reward. I thought that was really clever because it's peanuts in terms of money. But can you imagine the reaction if you're sitting at your desk and someone comes along with a balloon for you?'

Dyke adds that he consciously made time while director-general at the BBC to quietly celebrate with employees when something had gone well:

'The Monday following the concert we covered to celebrate the Queen's Jubilee, when the Queen guitarist Brian May had played on the roof of Buckingham Palace, I came into the office and sent a quick email to everyone just saying, "Wasn't that wonderful, didn't we do well?" Everyone felt like that on that day, but it's important to say it. It would be easy not to do it because you forget or are too busy, but it is important to do it, I think.'

Sue Campbell takes an even more proactive approach at her organization, UK Sport. Reward and acknowledgement of achievement and effort, she says, is vital to good leadership: 'If someone handles themselves really well in a meeting and stands up to a battering by someone, I will bang on their door and say well done, good job. I think that gives people a sense of accomplishment and it doesn't matter if you're six years old and a milk monitor or 60 years of age, its good reinforcement when someone says you've done a good job.' Campbell also introduced a star system at UK Sport which she says may call to mind memories of school days, but is nevertheless effective:

'Everyone is allowed to award their colleagues a star. Not for trivial things but if someone really goes the extra mile. The other day, someone here was ill and one of their colleagues dropped everything to take them home, then worked late to finish the job. They were given a star. It feeds into their appraisal system, so it does make a difference. And it's important to acknowledge human endeavour.'

The challenge for Dame Stella Rimington was that the work of her organization, MI5, does not allow for public recognition of success. 'It was a classic difficulty that the people in MI5 can't get credit for the things that have gone well – that wonderful secret operation that has successfully prevented something dreadful happening, tends to have to remain secret – whereas the failures are out there for everyone to see. It was important that people understood that from the moment they joined. One way of coping with that was to create a supportive family atmosphere. Everything I've said or done in trying to lead comes out of that. It is very important that people understand the culture, buy into it and then get all the support they need from within.'

MORALE

While good morale is important to any successful organization, to the armed forces it is absolutely critical. As Lord Inge puts it, an army without morale is nothing but a collection of unhappy, frightened men and women.

But what is morale? The Oxford English dictionary defines morale as 'the mental attitude or bearing of an individual or group, especially as regards confidence and discipline'. Viscount Slim, in his book[3], argues that morale is a state of mind and a mixture of emotion and logic. At its best, he says, high morale means that every individual in a group will give his last ounce of effort.

Colonel Bob Stewart says that 'morale is so closely linked to military leadership as to be almost indistinguishable. High morale and good leadership go hand-in-hand.' He explains using a quote famously attributed to Napoleon:

> 'Napoleon said that morale is to the physical as three is to one. That came home to me while I was in Bosnia. The local military commanders would come to me and ask me how many soldiers I had under my command. I would say, "Quite a lot. How many do you think I have?" They said they thought I had between 3000 and 4000. The truth was that I had 900.'

Lord Inge argues that the main ingredients of high morale are confidence, discipline and self-respect. He quotes Viscount Slim as arguing that morale must have strong mental, spiritual and material foundations. In other words, the forces need to believe in what they are doing, that what they are doing is important, that the aims are achievable, and that they are as well prepared as possible. A number of factors feed into this, such as good training, good and open communication, excellent back-up and living conditions, and the setting of high personal standards.

One significant complication is that the morale of troops can often depend to a large extent on factors that are outside the control of their leaders. Lord Inge argues that it is enormously important for the armed forces to feel that the nation is behind them: 'If you lose that, I think you have a problem.'

Major General Patrick Cordingley adds that soldiers also need to know that they have the best possible back-up should things go wrong:

'It's very important that the commander makes absolutely certain that everybody knows that if you are wounded, your chances of survival are very high. That means that you have to be very well trained. It means that your medical facilities have to be close to the point of wounding. It means that the casualty evacuation system has got to be very good. It means that the centre the injured are evacuated to has to be first-class. We spent a lot of time rehearsing [medical evacuations] and making absolutely certain that the soldiers knew that. So if they came back out from the desert, they knew that they could get to the field hospital in an hour and a half from the time of injury and that they would be very well looked after. Word got around.'

Major General Cordingley also stresses the importance of a leader's reaction during difficult or stressful situations as any suggestion of fear or despondency can travel easily in such a close-knit atmosphere. He tells of one evening in the run-up to the attack on Kuwait, when the Desert Rats had finished their final preparation exercise after five months in the desert and international negotiations with Iraq had reached a critical point:

'A message came over the air that there had been a breakthrough in the negotiations and Saddam was going to pull out of Kuwait. The relief I felt was just overwhelming. We had cracked it. I was sitting on top of my tank with the air streaming past and there were *tears of relief pouring down my cheeks. Fortunately, no-one could see because we were all driving along and it could easily have been mistaken for the effects of dust and sand. But of course within an hour we knew that it wasn't the case and Saddam was not going to pull out. That was the one moment when I really had to get a grip on myself, after a moment of huge euphoria. It was very difficult. And there were a lot of people around me who I knew felt the same. I had to work really hard the next day to pick people back up again. I went around the men saying remember, nothing has changed. Just forget what happened yesterday. I told them that the simplest way home was through Iraq and that was what we had to do. The soldiers knew exactly what that meant.'*

INSPIRATIONAL LEADERSHIP

Some organizations, particularly those in the creative industries, need something beyond motivational leadership if they are to perform at their best. Kevin Roberts, worldwide CEO of Saatchi & Saatchi, explains that his organization depends on the unleashing of ideas. As a result, his style of leadership, he says, is inspirational, rather than managerial. 'Inspiration is at the heart of today's leaders. I try to be inspirational in my language, in what I talk about and how I talk about things, in the way I connect with people. I hope that every interaction I have with someone inspires them to think about something in a different way or do something differently or achieve what they were trying to achieve when they came to see me. The key to great companies is to unleash your people and inspire them against a dream to be the best they can be.'

It is an approach that is unlikely to translate as effectively with every organization since Saatchi & Saatchi is a highly creative, ideas-driven business with a young and highly mobile workforce. Roberts explains how his workforce differs from many other organizations:

'I live in Tribeca in New York, very close to Citigroup's offices and I watch their employees funnel in in the morning and funnel out at night. My people don't funnel in at any time. They're all over the

place. They might be here at four o'clock in the morning. We are very young – our average age is 27 – and we have 20% turnover of staff every year, so I effectively have a new company every five years. Some people come and go many times because we attract passionate, restless people who want to be directors or open their own agency or have a crack at living in a different country. So they come back and then they go away and do it again and so on. And we think that in order to attract young people we need to attract dreamers. I value ideas massively and I put myself in situations where you will succeed and win through ideas and not through process, structure or hierarchy, although they are all important cogs in the world of business.'

Greg Dyke, the former director general of the BBC, would agree that a creative organization that both depends and thrives on ideas needs an inspirational working environment: 'The only thing that matters is good ideas. Man can go for three days without water and for 20 days without food but he can go a lifetime without a good idea. What you have to do is find the people with good ideas.'

Inspiring people so they are capable of achieving more than they thought possible, he says, is a key element of leadership. 'You have to make it exciting. It's about convincing people that they are capable of great things, more than they ever imagined.' Dyke believes that the key lies in creating an atmosphere where people are not afraid to take risks: 'You can only create that sort of environment by allowing people to get on with it and if it all goes wrong, so what? It's about fear. You have to reduce the fear in their lives.'

But how do you create an inspirational environment and then ensure that it can be sustained? While inspiration is something of a nebulous concept, Roberts and Saatchi & Saatchi take perhaps a more structured view towards the inspirational environment at the organization than you might expect. Roberts believes that inspirational leadership can and should be consciously developed and actively taught. 'Some people are born Mandela-like or Gandhi-like and others are not. You can nurture inspiration, you can demand it and you can coach it.' He explains the approach adopted at Saatchi & Saatchi:

'We look at it in four areas: shape, share, steer and sustain. Those are the areas where I think I need to be inspirational in. Obviously in today's world you have to shape your own destiny because if you are responsive and passive, you might as well say goodbye. The world is moving at speed and so is the competition. Shaping new ways of doing things and new answers is very important. I think sharing is vital because I simply do not believe in this hierarchical command and control, a structure that most US and UK businesses still follow. The role of a leader is to share a dream. We all want to work for something bigger than a pay cheque and bigger than producing a new laundry detergent. You've got to share a dream and then within that you've got to steer it, because the reality is that people have short attention spans. You've got problems you never thought of and new competitors you never saw coming. An inspirational leader has got to stay the course. Then you have to sustain it all in the face of great adversity because adversity is a way of life. And you have to do all those things in an inspirational way and not in a managerial way.

'The other thing we want to give our people is joy. These kids aren't going to stay at a company for five minutes if they are not loving it. Our parents' generation found no joy in most of their jobs. They didn't expect it, they didn't even look for it and they weren't disappointed when they didn't get it. This generation is different.

'So leaders have to create a situation where those things happen every day for every person in that enterprise. You've got to provide a space where people can gain responsibility, can be recognized, can work and can have fun.'

Greg Dyke also took positive steps to create a more inspirational atmosphere within his organization. When he joined the BBC, Dyke was faced with an organizational culture where, by the staff's own admission, it was difficult to be creative or innovative. To address this problem, he introduced a series of initiatives that were designed to encourage creativity to run free within the workforce as a whole and uncover ideas that might otherwise have remained hidden. Why, he argues, if the organization depended on new and creative ideas were those ideas only coming from producers, who were only a small proportion of the workforce? One of Dyke's initiatives was borrowed directly from the US. The 'watering hole' – so called because a watering hole is the one place in the jungle where all animals collect together to drink – is a place where anyone in the company can come and throw in an idea. Another was a number of conferences – which were deliberately held outside of London, where the BBC headquarters was based – where any staff member could present a programme idea:

'We held three of these big ideas conferences where anyone in the company could apply to come along. They came with the ideas and the controllers of the channels would be there. Some of the programme ideas were commissioned as a result. If you are in the accounts department and suddenly you can come up with an idea that has a chance of being commissioned, your whole view of the organization changes. I remember getting up to speak at one of them and the warmth of the applause was amazing. I thought, there's something very interesting happening here.'

THE ROLE OF ORATION

One of the misconceptions about leadership is that a good leader is always a good orator, and that the big occasions call for a driven, inspiring, motivating address to the crowds. Very few of our leaders admit to being good at, or even comfortable with, public speaking and almost all say that if they have to pull a big motivational speech out of the hat at a critical moment, it is only an indication that not enough preparation has been done in the run-up to that big event.

Nasser Hussain speaks for many leaders when he says that he would be disappointed if his team needed 'some tallyho speech from me on a Wednesday night in order for them to go out and be success-ful for England the next day'. Sir Clive Woodward agrees, and says that he is frequently asked about what he said to the English rugby team before the world cup final against Australia in 2003, as though a speech could have made all the difference between winning and losing in the moments before a key game:

> 'Speeches and motivation are very strange. When you win, people exaggerate what you said. When you lose, which you do more than win, people say, what happened to your motivational talk? All I said to the team was that it was just another game. They had to get all the other stuff that was going on out of their heads, get on the pitch and get back to the basics of the game. There was no need to tell them that this was the game of their life. If we played as well as we could, we would win. We would only lose if we got distracted.'

Woodward adds that his approach was mirrored by the team's cap-tain, Martin Johnson. One of the players commented after the World Cup final that it was a habit of Johnson's before every game to turn to the team as they walked down the tunnel onto the pitch and say something. Before the final, though, Johnson stopped in the tunnel, turned to the team as usual – and said nothing at all. 'The players said that was exactly what they needed,' says Woodward. 'Everyone knew what was at stake.'

Johnson himself says that he always tried to lead by example and was not given to tub-thumping speeches. 'It's not what you say to the team when you stand up in front of them, it's what you do every minute of every day when you're around them.' His brief talk to the players during the team meeting the night before the final was as low-key as Woodward's:

'What can you say? There's nothing you can say immediately before the World Cup final. The whole point is that it's the biggest game of your life and everyone knows that. I just told them not to do anything special and just to do what they always do. It's just another game of rugby, I said. We had beaten Australia four times by that stage, so we knew we could do it, but we also knew that if we didn't play well they could beat us. Sometimes the guys think you have to pull out a big game in order to win. We just had to do what we do.'

Major General Patrick Cordingley is one leader who did choose to make motivational speeches at critical moments. 'I don't think you have to be a good orator to be a good leader but it certainly helps,' he says. 'The most important thing is that you believe in what you are saying, because it will be obvious to everyone if you don't.' He says he did make at least one motivational address to his troops in the days before the Iraq war, saying he is simply 'of the age when I do tend to revert to being perhaps slightly over the top, and referring to past glories of the British Army'. He says that he told his men to recall the traditions of Monty's Desert Rats, and their contribution during the Second World War: 'I said we were back in the desert now and we were going to be proud of what we were doing. I was a bit theatrical, if you like, but I wasn't embarrassed by that.'

Generally, the leaders agree that underpinning the ability to motivate over the long term is a demonstrable dedication to a set of values. With a few very rare exceptions, it is not possible to be a good motivator unless you are already a good leader. In the next chapter we look at one of the most crucial elements of effective leadership – successful teamwork.

WHAT LEADERS REALLY DO:

- Create an atmosphere where employees feel valued and trusted
- Concentrate on creating a framework that allows employees to do their job efficiently
- Set challenging but achievable goals
- Delegate decisions downwards wherever possible
- Recognize and celebrate successes
- Allow people to take risks
- Rarely rely on motivational speeches.

---

[1] *What Leaders Really Do,* Harvard Business Review, p 86
[2] *What Leaders Really Do,* Harvard Business Review
[3] *Defeat Into Victory: Battling Japan in Burma and India*

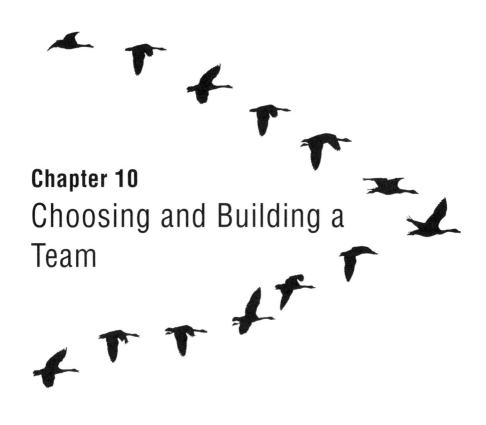

Chapter 10
Choosing and Building a Team

The man who occupies the first place seldom plays the principal part.

Johann Wolfgang von Goethe

Jack Welch, the legendary CEO of General Electric, once said that as CEO he had only three jobs: to select the right people, to allocate capital resources, and to spread ideas quickly. Modern leadership thought centres around the recognition that any organization has, potentially, many leaders and that the role of the ultimate leader is to recognize and nurture the wide variety of talent within the business. As Kotter says, 'with careful selection, nurturing and encouragement, dozens of people can play important leadership roles in a business organization.'[1]

The author and academic, Warren Bennis, founding chairman of the Leadership Institute at the University of California, believes that in the future, problems within organizations will be solved by 'task forces comprised of relative strangers who represent a set of diverse professional skills'. He argues that organizations are increasingly becoming federations where power is spread rather than centralized. Modern leaders, he says, understand what he calls 'the power of appreciation', where they can no longer make things happen, but only create an environment where people are encouraged to do good things.

The leaders we spoke to agree strongly that selecting the right people and encouraging them to perform well as a team is a vital element of their role. 'My view about going through this whole process is I will be OK if I have smarter people around me the whole time,' says Sebastian Coe. 'I don't think there are any happy accidents when it comes to project management and by and large you have the best chance of getting the project done if you have people with experience and intelligence around you.'

Dame Stella Rimington agrees: 'The first time I became a manager I realized that the most important thing to do is to make sure that you've got the best people and if that means stealing them from others, too bad. That is going to be the key to your success. You have to create something that people want to join and then the best people will gravitate towards you.' The England rugby player Jonny Wilkinson echoed this last point when he talked of the atmosphere that Sir Clive Woodward developed around the England team: 'Clive made it so when you had spent time training or playing with England and went back to your club, you couldn't bear the thought of never going back to play with England again.'

So what qualities do leaders look for in the people around them? Every leader has a different opinion, depending on the nature of the organization and their personal preferences. Ron Dennis, chief executive of McLaren, says simply that 'passion' is the main requirement: 'It's simple. You shouldn't even bother going through the door if you don't have passion about what we do.'

One of Warren Bennis' 10 principles for 'great groups' is that they hold a shared dream at their heart. Sebastian Coe looked for evidence of this shared vision when recruiting his team at the London Organising Committee for the Olympic Games and Paralympic Games. 'The people here have one thing in common. I asked them all the same question during their interview and that was, why do you want to do this? They all answered with variations on the same theme, which was "How could I not do this? I can't just sit and watch." These were all people who were walking away from senior jobs with big salaries and they all said they weren't going to lie on their deathbed and think "I wish I'd spent more time at Goldman Sachs". I didn't want to spend time with people who didn't get what this is all about.'

Heather Rabbatts says that in a challenging organization such as the Borough of Lambeth, she invariably looked for people who had the strength of character to cope with the difficult situations they might face. 'I needed people who were up for taking risks,' she says. 'I used to say to them that there is no point coming here if you are risk averse. You will be in the front line and I will always protect you but there's only so much I can do. My head of education at Lambeth, for instance, was a fantastic woman. We were closing schools at the time and she was out there, holding her own and talking to parents, teachers and politicians.'

Gail Rebuck of Random House says that since publishing is a people-based business, she looks for team members who are 'collegiate, with a degree of personal charm and the ability to get on with a wide range of people. That's absolutely essential. The perfect person would be someone who loves working in a team but at the same time can lead a team. Someone with real imagination and flair who enjoys thinking independently or as part of the team. Someone who will become part of the prevailing culture but add to it at the same time.'

THE POWER OF DIVERSITY

Many leaders recognize the importance of complementing their own skills and compensating for their weaknesses in their immediate team. 'No leader is an island,' says Field Marshal Lord Inge. 'No-one is so all-knowing that they don't need other people around them to make them understand some of the issues.' While the leaders invariably look for some common qualities in people, many actively seek out characters in their immediate team who will complement their own: 'You don't want a company of Kevin Robertses, that would just be awful,' says the worldwide CEO of Saatchi & Saatchi. 'One of the things I learned early on in my career from [the fashion designer] Mary Quant was that diversity is about competitive advantage, not political correctness.'

In a wider sense, the leaders showed a willingness to recognize and accept that individuals have different skills and abilities and that effective leaders embrace this diversity. Martin Glenn tells of a leadership course he attended while Roger Enrico was president of Pepsico:

'There were a dozen of us around a table on the first day and he asked each of us to explain the results of our 360 degree feedback reports. He started with Terry Ryan, a tough New Yorker from the sales side of the business. Terry said that his feedback was that he was strong on leadership but not so good with numbers. Roger stopped him straight away and said "Terry, you're crap with numbers and always have been. Your feedback hasn't changed in the past 10 years, and nor has mine." He asked whether anyone's feedback had changed. We all said no and he said, "Good." What we needed to understand was that we are who we are and we work to our strengths. We all have weaknesses and we try to deal with them but it is very hard to fundamentally change the way you are wired. The day Terry becomes good with numbers, he said, is the day he becomes bad at the parts of his job he's currently good at.'

While some leaders feel that effective decision-making requires a clear individual leader, others are able to work successfully in close partnership with colleagues and the boundaries of leadership become more blurred. When Nasser Hussain was appointed captain of the England cricket team in 1999, he had never met Duncan

Fletcher, who was appointed coach at the same time. Even so, their partnership turned out to be highly successful thanks, says Hussain, to their ability to dovetail their characters and skills. 'He came from a different world, the business world and I respected that. I was happy to have someone who was out of the norm. He brought a different angle on things, a management structure and a clarity of thought that said that if you do something today, there will be consequences three months or three years down the line.' Hussain adds that 'Fletch made me look like a better captain because tactically he was a genius, although he never pushed himself forward', and says that the mutual respect between the pair meant they were able to blur the boundaries between their roles. 'I didn't have a tick list and have to do everything as leader. There were days when I would be concentrating on my own game and Fletch would take over the lead role.'

Sir Clive Woodward says that the choice of captain is extremely important to the success of the team. 'You need to have someone who will take on board what you say and lead on it.' Woodward's captain, Martin Johnson, was 'brilliant', he says. 'If he had gone against anything I was trying to do, it wouldn't have worked.'

Hussain believes that every team has a 'heartbeat – the one player that the youngsters look up to and perhaps that the older ones are jealous of'. When appointed captain he assessed his team and quickly recognized Darren Gough as the heartbeat of the team. 'If I lost Gough I lost the team. When you're winning, everyone can look after themselves but when you're losing, it's different, people are talking in corners. But there was one voice that they would always listen to and that was him.' While he likes and respects the player, Nasser also recognized that it was important for his captaincy to have Gough as an ally:

'During my first tour, to South Africa, Gough was overweight. He knew it and so did I. At the first press conference one of the journalists said to me that he was looking overweight and ropey and hadn't taken a wicket in the run-up to the first test. So I said that Gough's was the first name I put on the team sheet and he always would be. He picked up on that straight away and ever since then

*has always backed me to the hilt. I knew that at some stage I would
have a bad patch with the team but I also knew that he would back
me through it. If you win his trust he has such a big heart that he'd
have to be steamrollered in order to change his mind.'*

Many leaders believe strongly that, as well as having complementary
skills, it is important that their immediate team feels able to question
and challenge their decisions. 'I'm always surprised that the nature
of the office of being chief executive means that, however you try to
infuse it with a different culture, people will step back from telling
you that a decision is crazy, partly through loyalty and partly because
they want to be cleared of any accountability,' says Heather Rabbatts. 'What I try to say is that loyalty is about trying to make the best
judgement calls in the interest of the organization, and sometimes I
won't get that right, so I need them all to think about how we do get
it right.'

'You have to encourage your team to challenge your decisions
because no-one's perfect,' agrees Sharkey Ward. 'If you have a team
of brilliant people working for you, their combined knowledge far
outweighs your own. You need to use everyone to solve a problem.'
Ward says he encouraged and appreciated feedback as squadron
commander: 'My senior pilot would occasionally come to me and tell
me that they thought I might have got something wrong and wanted
me to think about it again. Every single time it was resolved properly
and many times they were right. I'm happy to change direction if they
all think something's not right. That comes from the team respecting
you and you respecting the team. It's a two-way street.'

Sir Clive Woodward agrees that mutual 'trust and respect' are
essential when working as a team. 'You have to pick people you trust
to be around you. They have to be able to come to you and lay it on
the table and know that it will not affect your relationship. I do not
want to work with "yes men" because as a leader you need to have
honest feedback.'

Charles Dunstone of the Carphone Warehouse, though, makes
the interesting point that it is relatively easy for team members to
assume the leader is right, even when they suspect that they are not.

Dunstone, a keen adventurer, took part recently in a walking expedition to the North Pole and says it was an interesting experience to be part of a team rather than the leader. 'Your aim is not to let the rest of the team down, rather than trying to get them to do something in particular. What was really interesting was that my hobby is sailing so I am quite good at navigation, and at one point we went off course. I had a feeling that there was something wrong but I stopped questioning it because I had become a sheep rather than a leader. It was only after two days that I finally said, "Look, I think we're going the wrong way." And we were.'

TRUST

Good team work and effective leadership require, at some point, the leader to step away and trust that everyone will do their job. 'Once you have taken an organization to the point where it is truly professional and the ways of behaving are absolutely ingrained, you have to trust,' says Gail Rebuck. 'At that moment of trust there is a transfer of responsibility from the leader to the team. You know when it arrives and you have to leave them to it.' Rebuck recognizes that letting go is not always easy for a leader and says that it took time for her to learn to do it. 'There was a time when I tried to do everything myself and I was always hovering behind people, checking. I just couldn't let go. Luckily, I'm well beyond that now.'

'I don't believe that you employ high quality people and tell them how to do the job,' is how Sue Campbell puts it. 'My job is to make sure I've got the right team.' Campbell illustrates this point neatly with a story about her early career as a netball coach at Loughborough University:

'My idea of coaching at that point was very didactic. I had it all planned. I was shouting to them all the time. After we finished our sessions on the Tuesday night the rugby team were next on the field and their coach, Jim Greenwood, asked me if I wanted to watch him coach. I did and I could barely hear his voice on the pitch, he just quietly chatted to a few players. He asked me later in the pub

what I thought and I said, "Jim, you really need to project your voice a bit more."

'The next week he said to me that he wasn't going to shout but asked me to come over to the players so I could hear what he was saying. And he said to them "OK, you've regained possession and there are five minutes left. Show me three ways that you could get to the line." And I thought, poor man, he really should borrow some books about this stuff. Afterwards in the pub I asked him what he thought of my coaching and he said, interesting, but said he would leave me with one thought while he went to the bar. Where did I sit during the game? I sat on the bench, I said. And then I realized what he meant. I was coaching a decision-making game and yet I was making all the decisions for the players. That was, in many ways, the thing that has made the biggest difference to my working life and to my life in management. Great coaches train their players to be good decision-makers and trust their players to make the right decisions. The leader is always sitting on the bench.'

Heather Rabbatts identifies the same point when she says that she sometimes has to step back from providing answers for her team. 'There are some problems that I can work through quite quickly,' she says, 'but I know that it is important to allow people to get to the same point of their own accord, or with some help. I restrain myself from giving solutions, otherwise people just don't learn.'

Dame Stella Rimington believes that a reluctance to delegate is a relatively common problem for leaders in the commercial sector. 'Having the right structures in place is important,' she says. She adds that she personally has never had a problem delegating, which she puts down to having to juggle life as a single parent with a full-time job. 'My whole life has been a question of never having enough time so I had to develop that ability to divide things up into compartments, realize you can't do them all and so finding someone else to do some of it.'

Sharkey Ward adds that it is important that a leader demonstrates that they trust their team and that they are loyal to them and will back them up wherever necessary. 'I used to say to everyone who joined my squadron from the most junior member of the squadron upwards that I knew they were good at their job so I wasn't going to waste time looking over their shoulder. It was fine if they wanted to ask my advice and I accepted that they were going to make mistakes, but as long as it was an honest mistake, they didn't need to worry about it. Just get it right the second time around. That approach really worked. They were a happy bunch of guys and when something did go wrong, they weren't afraid to tell me.'

He adds that this meant overlooking the occasional indiscretion – he made it clear from the outset, for instance, that if one of the pilots had overdone a celebration the night before, they should come and see him. 'They did occasionally and I would say fine, no problem, go and sleep it off and we'll see you tomorrow. I kept no record of it and they knew there were no hard feelings. In order to get that trust and loyalty upwards you have to display it downwards. That's the most important thing in a team.' Ian Mortimer, a member of Sharkey's squadron for many years, agrees: 'One of the best things about him was how positive he was about his people. He was fiercely loyal to his team.'

DEVELOPING FUTURE LEADERS

Delegation and trusting a team to perform independently has another benefit, of course. Many of the leaders make the point that part of their role is to identify and encourage future leaders to develop within the organization, and an effective way to do that is to pass responsibility onto others in a supportive environment. 'Successful corporations don't wait for leaders to come along,' said John Kotter in *What Leaders Really Do*. 'They actively seek out people with leadership potential and expose them to career experiences designed to develop that potential.'

Kevin Roberts at Saatchi & Saatchi believes strongly in giving people responsibility early and allowing them to make mistakes. 'How do leaders grow?' he asks. 'Good judgement comes from bad judgement; it doesn't come from being told what to do. You don't learn to walk by listening to your dad and watching how he does it. Babies learn to walk by falling over and thinking, that hurt. I'm not going to fall over again.'

Good leaders recognize the importance of recruiting and nurturing staff who will take the organization into the future. Heather Rabbatts says that she always tries to identify 'people with potential, who are ripe for the next challenge, and then put them in a project team and see how they work'. She also likes to place people in teams that are outside of their comfort zone and require different elements of expertise than they have displayed in the past. 'I think that's a good thing to do,' she says.

Sue Campbell takes a more formalized approach to developing talent in her organization and says that everyone at UK Sport has their own personal improvement plan. 'I'm a great believer that everyone in a company should have their own individual and personalized programmes of support,' she says. 'It could be attending courses; it could be peer mentoring, or something else. I want every person in this building to be the best they can possibly be, and then I know that the company will be the best it can be.'

PREPARING FOR SUCCESS

Success is rarely an accident. In business as well as sport, the people who come out on top are generally those that have put in the most work. 'You can't make it up when you get there,' says Martin Johnson, captain of the World Cup-winning England rugby team. 'You can't make up the fitness work you've put in, or the work ethic within the team. It has to be there already and with us, it was.'

A talented team, in any field, will have trouble producing their best if they are placed in an inefficient working environment. The leader's role is to create an atmosphere and environment where their people can produce their best endeavours.

It is widely acknowledged that Sir Clive Woodward's overriding achievement as coach of the England rugby team was to put in place the support framework and the levels of preparation that allowed the team to become the best in the world. When England arrived in Australia at the start of the World Cup tournament in 2003, they were not only the fittest English team to play at the tournament, they were also the best-prepared and supported. They had achieved world number one-ranked status two seasons earlier. Woodward managed and coached the team and had found the best coaches to work with the players on every facet of the game, including an attack coach, defence coach, throwing coach, kicking coach, line-out coach and even an eye coach, whose task it was to train the players to see the ball as efficiently as possible. 'I gave the team the best coaches and everything they needed to deliver,' says Woodward. In other words, the players had done all of their hard work in training and by the time the World Cup arrived, at that stage they just needed to play.

Preparation is vital in any sport. The former England cricket captain Nasser Hussain says that one of his coaches used to say 'it's not the work you do off the field that is important, it is just knowing that you have done more than the opposition.' The more you practice, he says, the luckier you get. 'And you have the added bonus of knowing mentally that you are well prepared.' Under Duncan Fletcher and Nasser Hussain, the English cricket team introduced a new level of preparation and training into the team's regime that covered diet, gym-based training and the wellbeing of the team in general. This professional approach to the game, says Hussain, paid dividends on the pitch.

The military leaders we spoke to make similar observations about the levels of preparation and support within the Armed Forces. 'Training is fundamental,' says Field Marshal Lord Inge. 'If you don't get the foundations right in peace time and you suddenly go to war, you get in a hell of a muddle.' The first thing to suffer if forces do not feel well trained, he says, is morale. Major General Patrick Cordingley makes the same point when he says that the most important thing he could impress on his men in the run-up to the first Gulf War was that the British Army was far better trained, prepared and supported than the enemy they would face. 'An army marches on its stomach,' is how Colonel Bob Stewart puts it. 'I used to say to the soldiers that unless we were well-administered we would not be able to do our job.'

TEAMSHIP RULES AND PROFESSIONALISM

Sir Clive Woodward believes strongly that a world-class team should look and behave like a world-class team. One of the initiatives he introduced early on during his career as coach of the England team would come to be called the 'critical non-essentials'. This meant that the team always looked well turned-out – their off-the-pitch suits were designed by Hackett – and the team had an agreed set of rules covering their behaviour on and off the pitch. 'You are not going to win the World Cup because you have a better uniform than anyone else, or because you arrive on a bus with the English rose on the side of it, but when you add everything up, it makes a difference,' says Woodward.

Duncan Fletcher took a similar approach while coach of the English cricket team, although initially the idea did not gain widespread approval. 'The only thing that Fletcher and I did not completely agree upon was that it would help us beat Australia if we all wore the same jackets,' says Nasser Hussain. Fletcher's argument, though, was identical to Sir Clive Woodward's: if a team looks and appears professional, people believe that it is a well-run organization. 'Anything that makes you feel or look like a team is not a hardship,' says Hussain. 'If it gives you an extra 1%, that's fine. Victory can come from that extra 1%.' A uniform or, in the England team's case, the ceremonial presentation of a cap when a player had completed a certain number of games, was important for creating a sense of belonging within the team, says Hussain. 'It doesn't matter what it is, as long as it makes you feel that it is your team.'

Hussain explains that the cricket team's sponsor at the time, Vodafone, told the team that they would provide extra money that would allow the team to have their own single hotel rooms while on tour (the players previously shared), visits from their wives while playing abroad and more preparation time for the national side. In return, the team was required to look immaculate. 'We would be well-dressed and shaved and turn up on time wherever we went and go to High Commission functions,' says Hussain. 'They said that they would provide the best gear for us and we would dress like the best team in the world. Most of us bought into that idea.' The players who were less keen, he adds, were asked to contribute to decisions. 'We put the ball into their court and set the rules ourselves.'

As well as the team's overall appearance, the England rugby team also developed and insisted on a highly professional set of behavioural rules. These were written down in the 'black book', although Martin Johnson says that the players rarely referred to the book because the rules were so ingrained in their everyday actions.

Crucially, says Sir Clive Woodward, these teamship rules were written and agreed upon by the players, before being signed off by the coach. One of the rules concerned timekeeping which for the players, meant not just being on time for the frequent meetings held for the team, but being 10 minutes early. Good timekeeping quickly became a matter of pride for the team, says Sir Clive:

> *'The players I see now still talk to me about timekeeping because I used to go potty about it. It's about standards. If anyone came into the room late we wouldn't say, you're late, we'd say, you've just cost us the World Cup. That is how single minded you have to be about it. The little things add up. You spend five years of your life preparing for the World Cup and if you arrive five minutes late with no excuse, then you've lost us the Cup. No-one was late, ever.'*

TEAM SPIRIT

Martin Johnson, who has more experience of operating within a team than most leaders, says that a team is formed at the point when 'you trust all the guys to do their job. I had days when I would turn up for training feeling tired or not at my best and I would look around the team and think, I can't let these players down. That was one of the things we used to often say before a game. We'd go into a circle and say, look around. Who is going to let this team down? And there was no-one who would. There was no-one there that we would have to look out for.'

As Johnson points out, though, the experience a world-class rugby team goes through is guaranteed to create strong bonds: 'You couldn't tell us much about being a team because by the World Cup we had been together a long time and had been through some serious stuff. We had played against South Africa in their own country and sat in a hotel knowing that there were 80,000 Afrikaners outside, baying for our blood.' He adds that the physical nature of the game means that players will automatically form a close bond. 'If I don't look after our front row during a scrum, they are going to get hurt. It's the same with lineouts – I have to trust the players to lift me properly or I'm going to get hurt. There's a bond there that is stronger than anything you can build from your average team bonding sessions.'

Sir Clive Woodward makes the point, though, that while only 15 players were in the team for the World Cup final, the behaviour of the rest of the 30-strong squad was as vital to success as the perform- ance on the pitch. He explains the reaction of the players in the five days between the naming of the team that would play Australia and the final itself. 'The reality when you name the final team for the World Cup final is that you have 15 players who are on the ceiling because they're in the team, another seven who are OK because they will be on the bench, and eight guys who are on the floor because they won't be taking part,' he says. 'How the team reacted at that moment could have lost us the World Cup. The real heroes in Australia were the eight players who were not in the final team. They trained with the rest of the team that week and put everything into it. They were never late for a single meeting. That's a team.'

Martin Johnson explains this by saying that the team was not one full of individual egos, but instead had a collective ego. This is another of Warren Bennis' 10 principles of great groups – that they manage conflict by abandoning individual egos in the pursuit of the dream.

Business leaders often struggle with the question of how to make everyone in an organization feel that they are important to its ulti- mate goals. 'It's like that well-worn story of the US President taking a tour of NASA,' says Ron Dennis of McLaren. 'He met a guy who was sweeping a corridor and asked him what his role was in NASA and the guy said, "I'm here to put a man on the moon".' Dennis' approach, particularly in the early days of McLaren, was to make sure that everyone in the company was present at the debriefing session when the team won or lost a Grand Prix. 'There was no-one there who should feel that they didn't contribute because they all do. They all contribute,' he says.

Sebastian Coe takes a similar approach at the London Organising Committee for the Olympic and Paralympic Games. 'I don't want to hear that the person sitting on reception has any less responsibility here than the Director of Operations. In fact, it is the person on reception that will probably field the phone calls from the President of the International Olympics Committee, so everyone is in this together.'

Heather Rabbatts is another leader who believes 'very strongly that you should value people for their contribution and not for their position in the hierarchy. Just because you are senior doesn't mean you have to behave in a certain way. I have as much time for people who are junior as I do for people who are more senior and I really instil that in my managers. I suppose I am very keen to get that sense of sharing in an organization.'

While director-general of the BBC, Greg Dyke's approach to making sure that everyone in the organization felt part of the same team began with the induction process for new recruits:

'Everyone had to go on an induction programme and most people who got a job with the BBC were quite excited about working for the organization, so we wanted to keep hold of that. So we used to take about 120 people at a time and go to watch the news being broadcast, or go to the Top of the Pops studio. Something that said, you are part of this, even if you don't work in this department. The other bonus of doing it that way was that the people on the course got to know each other and created another network so, once they were working in the organization, they would ring each other up when they needed something rather than sending each other crap memos.'

In general, the leaders' approach to teamwork illustrates the changing nature of leadership from the old command and control format. Many leaders see their role as preparing others to perform as well as they can and are prepared, wherever necessary, to take a back seat.

WHAT LEADERS REALLY DO:

- Place the utmost importance on selecting the best people
- Surround themselves with people who have complementary skills to their own
- Actively develop future leaders
- Look for and encourage a shared vision within a team
- Transfer decision-making downwards wherever possible
- Encourage people to find their own answers, rather than provide them
- Demonstrate trust and loyalty
- Value everyone in the team equally for their contribution.

---

[1] *What Leaders Really Do* Harvard Business Review December 2001

Chapter 11
Communication

Drowning in data yet starved of information.

Ruth Stanat

Strong communication skills are accepted as one of the main essential characteristics of a good leader. But, as Rob Goffee and Gareth Jones point out,[1] there is more to it than that. 'Skilful leaders ensure that they use the right mode of communication,' they say. 'This requires a fine appreciation of the message, the context, the people you wish to communicate with, as well as your own personal strengths and weaknesses.'

There are two distinct but connected elements to communication when it comes to leadership. One is the vital process of communicating the overall vision or strategy throughout the organization, which

we discussed in Chapter 4. The other element is the everyday interaction that the leaders have with employees, other stakeholders, the
public and press, and it is this element that we will concentrate on in
this chapter.

Martin Johnson, captain of the England rugby team that won the
World Cup in 2003, neatly characterizes the distinction between
these two elements of communication as 'big talk, little talk'. Communication of strategy, vision and, in the case of rugby, overall match
tactics, he calls 'big talk'. 'Little talk', by contrast, is the everyday
conversation with people around you. Little talk encourages people,
it gives them confidence and reassurance, and it motivates them. On
the rugby pitch, says Johnson, the team are constantly talking to each
other, letting each other know where they are and what they plan to
do. 'Little talk,' says Johnson, 'makes the big talk happen.'

TOO MUCH TALK?

The leaders we spoke to had differing views on the 'right' level of
communication. Nasser Hussain, for instance, says that 'less is more.
If, as a captain, you are constantly talking, the message becomes
diluted. Some of the greatest people I have listened to don't say
much at all. Graham Thorpe is like that. If he says something at a
team meeting everyone will be listening because he won't have said
anything at the previous six.' Martin Johnson makes the additional
point that good communication does not necessarily mean verbal
communication: 'Body language is very important as well. Phil Vick-
ery is a great communicator when he is on the field, just in the way
he holds himself.'

In large organizations, however, the challenge for leaders is to
remain as visible as possible, and to be perceived as being as accessible as possible to a large number of employees who may be scattered
across the globe. The larger the organization, the greater the communication challenge that the leader faces. Kevin Roberts is worldwide
chief executive of an organization, Saatchi & Saatchi, that has 7000
employees in 83 countries and he uses every possible medium of
communication:

'I write blogs and make videos for the intranet. I have my own web-site. And I spend 250 days of the year on the road. I visit around 40 offices every year. I take part in a lot of Q&A sessions and people can also take part in Q&As on my website. It's so easy to stay in touch these days because technology is so interactive.

'The important point to remember with communication is that telling is not sharing. Most of the corporate communication I see is one-way – from the big shots to the little shots. My stuff is much more two-way and interactive. I want people to ask me, tell me; say what they think. Everything they want to know but may be afraid to ask. I've been here nine years now so everyone is used to that.'

The one form of communication that Roberts does not routinely use, interestingly, is email, on the grounds that if he did, he would never have time to do anything else. 'I get maybe 600 emails a day,' he says. 'My secretary sorts through them and prints them out and then I write on them by hand and she scans them and sends them back. Everyone who needs one gets a written response. That means it's short, but personal and it's over quite quickly so you don't get caught into email mania.'

Greg Dyke, on the other hand, made widespread use of email as a communication tool while he was director-general of the BBC, although he stresses that it is important that every email you send is interesting. 'Email is wonderful in many ways because it allows you to communicate with everyone at once. The problem is that some people don't communicate, but send out boring stuff.'

He adds that email was invaluable in a large organization like the BBC, which was constantly under the public spotlight and frequently mentioned in the press. 'In an organization like the BBC it is impor-tant to share things that matter with the staff before they read about it in the papers,' he says. Email gave him the means to make the employees feel included in the organization, even when they were located far from the head office. Dyke was always careful to take the time to send out a celebratory email when something went well, and always to be sure that he wrote the messages himself and that they were something that people would want to read:

> *'That was the point. I was a journalist so I can write. If you send out messages that are full of management gobbledygook or something turgid about what happened at the World Service last week, you are dead. No-one will read it and once they stop, [in an organization of that size] you have no impact on them as a leader.*

> *'Email is wonderful for swift, sharp messages. The interesting thing for me was that when I first got to the BBC and started sending emails, I got feedback from them because there are a lot of young people in the organization and that is what they do. It is so important that everyone knows what is going on and I think that is what my predecessors failed to understand. Chris Patten, who used to be governor of Hong Kong, came up to me at an event one day and said, don't stop sending those emails. It turned out that his daughter worked for the BBC and she had told him about them. This is a small world and if everyone goes home or out to a dinner party and moans about the BBC, that's incredibly damaging to the organization. Instead, if they go home and say it's great, and that means that we are getting somewhere.'*

Charles Dunstone, co-founder and chief executive of the Carphone Warehouse, has had to adapt his communication style and methods as the company has grown. He relies on email to keep in touch with what is going on at the coalface, in the stores. 'I get a lot of emails from people working at the stores,' he says. 'If something is going wrong they tell me, they know I would want to know.' He adds that email allows him to include as many of his employees as possible in the plans for the business. 'Quite often if I'm thinking of doing something I send an email out to ask people what they think. It's a great thing if you can ask that question because then when it eventually happens, people feel that they have been consulted. The problem as you get bigger, though, is that email can be quite leaky so I have to write the emails, to some extent, imagining that they might appear in a newspaper. I hate that because it's not how it used to be.'

Heather Rabbatts also found communication a challenge when she was chief executive of the London Borough of Lambeth, particularly since she wanted to encourage interaction with the employees, rather than a series of one-way messages. 'There's a really important difference between communication and information,' she says. 'We are all human beings and what we want is a conversation, and that is a real challenge in a large organization.' While at Lambeth she would meet with the 250 senior managers every six weeks, as well as collecting together groups of staff from different divisions and services, but says that talking to all 10,000 employees at once was just not feasible.

> 'There are all sorts of information pathways through which you can try and keep people informed but that is a very different experience from feeling that you have had a conversation. So I used to pick 20 or so people from all sorts of different parts of the Authority and sit down and have a chat with them over lunch. I think it's important to try and find ways of maintaining [that intimacy] in a large organization, and that is a really big challenge. Technology helps in informing people but you still need to find a way of having that conversation.'

AUTHENTIC COMMUNICATION

Goffee and Jones argue that there is no correct level or form of communication, but that each leader should play to their own strengths and weaknesses and choose a communication strategy that works for them: 'While face-to-face communication will always be important for leaders, it is also necessary for them to consider how to connect directly and effectively with larger audiences.'[2]

Inevitably, being a leader calls for at least the occasional foray into large-scale oration. It is not, by any means, a situation that all leaders feel comfortable with but the leaders we spoke to have generally learned how to be effective at public speaking within their own particular boundaries of comfort and ability. As Major General Patrick Cordingley puts it, 'You don't need to be a great orator to be a successful leader, but I would say that it certainly helps.'

Heather Rabbatts is one of the relatively few leaders who are comfortable with speaking at large events, a fact she puts down to her training as a barrister. 'I'm one of those people who can speak in front of 3000 people without notes,' she says. 'I'm absolutely fine about it. It's a great skill to have, although it took me a while to realize that.' She adds that it is possible for someone who is not a great orator to still have an impact at a large event and says that the secret, for her, is to speak with confidence. 'I used to say to people, if you don't know the answer, just say it with confidence and that will make a difference. Don't say "I don't really know", but "I don't really know the answer to that question but this is how we are going to find out". People are more willing to accept that.'

Charles Dunstone of the Carphone Warehouse freely admits that he was extremely uncomfortable with speaking at big events in the early days of the company, but has grown used to it. 'I think probably the greatest thing I discovered in communication, which is missed by many people, is humility,' he says. 'People hate it when someone stands up and gives it the big "I am". If you approach it with a good deal of humility and sympathy for your audience and if you are honest about how you have been lucky and so on, then that makes an enormous difference. And that's when you talk to people, not at people.'

For Sue Campbell, the secret to successful communication is to be 'unbelievably well-prepared. I may not look as though I am – it might look as though I just stand up and talk, because I never use notes when I speak. But I am always incredibly well-prepared. I never go into anything unprepared.' Campbell adds that one of the elements that makes her effective as a communicator is that she is not afraid to ask questions, even if they seem to be obvious. 'I wouldn't say that I'm that intellectual so I've learned to simplify in order to explain. Sometimes I drive people mad because I keep asking them to explain things to me one more time until I get it. I have to have things at a level that I can interpret. And that allows me to be a good communicator.'

Not everyone is happy talking to a large group of people – many leaders prefer to try and get their message across through smaller groups. That said, even the leaders who are comfortable talking to large groups frequently say that smaller groups are much more effective.

Major General Patrick Cordingley led a brigade of around 5000 troops during the first Gulf War. He says that once the plan was clear and a rough timetable for the advance into Kuwait had been established, he set himself the task of talking to each soldier in groups of no more than 100:

> 'It is only in smaller groups like that that you can get decent eye contact with people and that is just what they want in a situation like that. What I wanted to impress on them was that they were extremely well trained and well equipped and although people were frightened and nervous, there was no need to be because we were in a far better state than the opposition. Smaller groups also gives them a fair chance to ask questions, which you must give them the opportunity to do because that is an important part of the process of them believing in what you are saying. If you have a group of no more than 100 you can probably take 10 or 15 questions.'

Dame Stella Rimington believes that communicating to a large group can be effective, if only to allow people to see the leader and hear what they have to say. But, she adds, even though some people will ask questions and raise issues at these meetings, others will 'go away and mutter in a corner'. That is why it is important, she says, for a leader to foster a situation where people 'are prepared to tell you about the mutterings, rather than just what they think you want to know'.

In general, the female leaders we spoke to tend to favour a collegiate form of leadership. Sue Campbell of UK Sport actively uses small consultative groups in order to encourage an atmosphere where people feel confident enough to ask the right questions. 'Groups give people confidence,' she says. 'If I just appear and talk it's difficult to know what I'm thinking and people may be unsure about whether they can challenge me or not. Often I'll set out an agenda then go and have a coffee and leave them to talk. When I come back often they will have formed a view and feel confident enough to have a better go at you.'

HONESTY AND INTEGRITY

As we have already seen, the leaders believe strongly that honesty and integrity lies at the core of good leadership. John Kotter backs up this view by arguing that messages are not necessarily accepted just because they are understood. In order for people to buy into the message, the leader has to have credibility. Many things, says Kotter, contribute to the credibility of the leader, including the consistency between the message and his or her actions, the content of the message itself, and the leader's reputation for trustworthiness and integrity.

Heather Rabbatts argues that honesty is often the best way out of any situation, however difficult. 'I am endlessly surprised by the fact that people think that being defensive is the best way to get through a difficult situation,' she says. While vice chair of Millwall Football Club, she faced a potentially volatile situation when the ticketing system failed during the team's first home game:

> *'We had hundreds of people queuing in the baking sun and my security adviser told me not to go out there or they might tear me limb from limb. So I said, don't be ridiculous and we went out into the crowd and said, sorry, the computer system has gone down. We're doing everything we can. It's always better to go out and talk to people in a situation like that. Always. Just admitting that you are in a mess and that you are sorting it out wins you the moment. It often wins you enough time to put things right. Not always, but often. On this occasion we put the kick-off back and by the time the game started there were around 50 fans still outside, so we let them in for free.'*

The military leaders we spoke to felt particularly strongly that it was important to be as honest as possible with their men, however blunt the message may be. The former chief of defence staff, Field Marshal Lord Inge, says the 'why' is the most important part of the message in a conflict situation. 'When you go to war, which is the most difficult decision any government ever has to make, you have to understand the reason for it. At the most dramatic end of the spectrum you are asking people to risk their life. You have to explain why. It's very important.'

Colonel Bob Stewart agrees and says 'you must always tell soldiers the truth'. He followed this rule when he led his forces into Bosnia as part of the UN peacekeeping force. Colonel Stewart had already been told that the casualty rate in Bosnia could be high, and he passed the information on to his men. 'I stood up in front of my battalion and told them that I had been told that each of us had a 25% chance of coming back wounded or in a box. That was the truth. And I said that if anyone did not want to come with me in that battalion they should say so now. No-one did.'

Naturally, there are occasions where it is not possible, or perhaps the best option, to be completely honest. Dame Stella Rimington, as director-general of MI5, was perhaps faced with more of those situations than many other leaders. 'Of course there are occasions where you can't be completely open and I found those quite difficult to manage. But they do happen. There are circumstances where you can't reveal your entire hand because to do so would scupper whatever you are trying to do from the outset.' She adds that it is easy in these situations for people to pick up on the fact that they are not being given the full story. 'People pick up on these things and begin to suspect that you are not communicating properly. It always happens when you can't put all of your cards on the table.'

Major General Patrick Cordingley had direct experience of this when he was faced with a complicated situation in the run-up to the first Gulf War. After his troops had left for training in the Gulf, he received information that the ammunition they carried in their tanks was much more volatile than anyone had previously believed:

'I was told that I couldn't tell anyone but they wanted me to tell the men to re-stow the ammunition in the tanks so that these more volatile charges were not stored next to each other. That way if the tank was hit and one went off, there was a sporting chance that the combustion could be stopped. The new, safer ammunition would be sent to us within a month. I said fine, but my soldiers aren't stupid. They understand what the risks are and they will see that something is wrong. I have to tell them why. I was told again that I could not.

'So I had to make a decision and I decided to ignore the order and keep the ammunition stored as it was. Of course I had considerable doubts about whether I had done the right thing, particularly when we were doing live firing exercises and I knew that if one of the tanks was hit there was a danger it could blow up completely. In the end I shared the problem with someone even though I had been told not to. I'm not saying that a problem shared is a problem halved but on this occasion, it was wonderful to get it off my chest.'

COMMUNICATING OUTSIDE THE COMPANY

For some organizations, particularly those with any political association, communication with and the perception of the companies by outsiders are as important as communication within the organization. Dame Stella Rimington, former head of MI5, says that 'external positioning' is one of the leader's most important roles, which in MI5's case meant gathering support from the government and the press. 'Only a leader can do that. An organization can be undermined if you are not managing that side of it all of the time. During times of change or threat that could take as much as 40% of my time and I would guess that these days, it would be much more.'

Sebastian Coe, chairman of the London Organising Committee for the Olympic and Paralympic Games, says that talking with the local communities that will be directly affected by the Games is crucial to his organization. Many leaders point out that it is important to keep repeating the overall vision or strategy internally within the organization because it takes so long for the message to seep through to all levels. For Coe, the problem is magnified greatly because the message has to be spread through the local community, the country, and beyond. 'Long after we become bored of the message there will be people out there who have never heard of it,' he says. 'It's very important that we hold on very firmly to the concept of this being a campaign. We need to keep people excited, not just in London but throughout the UK. We also have to manage their expectations so they don't think that East London is going to wake up to nine new sport complexes by Christmas. Communication is absolutely at the heart of this.'

He adds that managers and leaders need to be careful in the language they use when spreading a message beyond the organization: 'Because we are so close to the issue we tend to use shorthand and talk about regeneration and sustainable communities, but people don't know what we mean by that. So we talk about people living in nice houses, we talk about clean rivers and we talk about young people enjoying sport. Once we made ourselves relevant to people, they started taking notice.'

DEALING WITH THE MEDIA

In this media-intensive world, the press – and the way press attention is managed – can wield an enormous amount of power over an organization. It invariably falls to the leader of the organization to play the most significant PR role.

While he was captain of the English cricket team, Nasser Hussain took the view that keeping the press onside was vital to his future. 'In the end, it is the press that will get any captain in sport. If they start going in one direction they won't let go,' he says. 'I used to give the press as much time as possible and answer all of their questions honestly and treat them all as though they knew everything about cricket. I knew that the minute you crossed them, they would remember, so I always gave them everything they needed.'

While his company has a communications team, Charles Dunstone of the Carphone Warehouse believes that it is important for him, as leader of the organization, to have a direct relationship with the press. He says that he takes calls from reporters he knows himself whenever possible. 'I think it's important that I have a dialogue with them.' He recognizes, though, that the attention focused on the company's Talk Talk broadband service grew from the fact that bad news makes for a good story. 'What is disappointing is that there are so many commentators out there who just wait for people to trip up. People have to take risks and try new things or the world will never change. We screwed up and I stood up and said sorry, but people just wouldn't leave it alone.'

Dunstone makes the additional point that his role as the PR figurehead has changed over the short life of the company: 'When you are the challenger in a sector, the company needs a public face and it needs that leg-up you get from PR. But later on when the company matures and becomes more of an established institution I think the leader should step back a bit and allow the company to speak for itself.' As a result, he has consciously stepped back out of the limelight. 'I still get written about and I can't avoid that, but my other rule is that I never do anything of a public nature that isn't to do with the business.'

Dunstone's experience at Carphone Warehouse is in direct contrast to the situation Dame Stella Rimington was placed in when director-general of MI5. She was, famously, the first director-general whose identity was openly announced to the press on appointment. The result was a concentrated media focus on the leader of the organization, rather than the organization itself. 'It has been said that there was too much focus on me as leader of the organization but that was inevitable, given that I was the first MI5 leader to be named and that I am a woman,' she says. 'Once the decision had been made, and it was made before I got the job, it was impossible to retreat from that personal focus.'

The new culture of openness that was slowly introduced at MI5 had major consequences for how the organization, and its leader, approached internal and external communication. 'Before, we had very little communication with the outside world, which meant, for example, that if there was any press comment or criticism the management was not able to respond,' Rimington explains. 'If it was wrong or unfair, as not surprisingly it often was, the staff felt aggrieved because the Service was being criticized unfairly and no one was standing up for them.'

The leaders we spoke to say that communication, in all its forms, is by far the most significant demand on their time. Inevitably, one of the most difficult aspects of leading an organization is effective time management and in the next chapter we discuss how the leaders create the time and space to reflect and recharge.

WHAT LEADERS REALLY DO:

- Encourage discussion and two-way conversations
- Share, rather than tell
- Prize honesty and openness
- Ensure their own communications with staff are interesting and meaningful
- Adapt their communication style and approach according to their own skills and personality
- Use technology when communicating with large organizations, but with care
- Tailor the message to the audience
- Tend to favour communicating to smaller groups
- Take ownership of external communication.

---

[1] *Why Should Anyone Be Led by You?* p 161
[2] *Why Should Anyone Be Led By You?* p162

Chapter 12
Looking After No 1

Leadership and learning are indispensable to each other.

John F Kennedy

Leadership is invariably a highly pressurized role. So how do leaders ensure that they have enough time to reflect and to recharge when they need it? In this chapter we look at the ways in which our leaders take steps to ensure that they retain their enthusiasm and sense of perspective, and create space for themselves to think and improve their leadership skills.

Being a leader is a lonely job, full of lonely decisions. Of course leaders – those who are not megalomaniacs, at least – are beset by self-doubt. As Sue Campbell says, 'anyone who tells you that they do not have self-doubt does not have self-awareness', although admitting freely and publicly to occasional bouts of anxiety does not come easily to everyone. Generally, it has to be said, female leaders are happier to admit to moments of self-doubt than male leaders.

Heather Rabbatts says that occasional doubts can sometimes be seen as 'really important insights' but adds that it is important to anyone to have people around 'to refuel you' after a personal crisis of confidence. For a leader, though, that is not always possible. 'When you are a leader very few people tell you that you are doing a good job,' says Rabbatts. 'You don't often get that level of reassurance. I've never had a coach or a mentor but I do feel that it is important for me to have somewhere to go in order to handle some of those doubts.' Rabbatts says she relies on good friends outside of the organization to act as a sounding board. 'These are lonely positions,' she says. 'You have to have a trusted space, somewhere to go.'

All of the leaders we spoke to admitted to finding their role intensely pressurized and all took steps, consciously or unconsciously, to create time and space to reflect on their decisions from time to time. Some make the point that it can be difficult to stay in touch with the grass roots of an organization when you are in a leadership role, and so it is important not to get caught up in the whirlwind of work. 'One of the dangers of leadership roles is that the job can grind you down,' says Greg Dyke. 'You don't have enough time to find good new ideas.' The most important lessons he has learned, he says, is to take regular holidays, 'not to think that you have to do it all' and not to 'read all the crap that you receive'.

'Finding time is very important,' agrees Field Marshal Lord Inge, 'not necessarily time for yourself to think but just time to sit down with someone and check that everything is OK with the men. It can be quite difficult at times – there were occasions when I felt I was chasing my own tail. But you do have to try and find the time. Sometimes 10 minutes is enough.'

Time management is invariably a challenge for leaders, irrespective of the type or organization they run. Many had developed their own tricks for managing time over the course of their career. Sir Clive Woodward, for instance, says that when he ran his own leasing company he learned a valuable lesson from some management consultants:

> *'These two Americans came in and analysed my business, took it apart. When they had finished the biggest lesson that came through to me was when they said that I needed a driver. It was the simplest thing – I could sit in the back of the car and work. That is one of the best things I have ever done and now, whenever I have to go on a long journey I hire a driver and have two or three hours in the back of the car, working. That's a huge amount of time. It might look flash but it does allow me to work.'*

Meetings are invariably the biggest potential waste of time for anyone in a leadership position. Again, the leaders we spoke to use a variety of techniques to ensure that valuable time is not swallowed up in a meeting that goes nowhere. The former chief of defence staff, Field Marshal Lord Inge, says that he became adept at reducing complicated briefs to a few short but critical points. 'It's very important that you have the questions you need answered clearly in your mind before you go to a meeting,' he says. Nasser Hussain says he and the coaches of the England cricket team took a similar approach during his time as captain. 'We believed in getting things sorted out before the meeting started. We would go in and try and sell our plan to the team, although they could disagree or suggest something else.' Overall, in common with other leaders, the secret to a successful meeting is structure, he adds.

Sir Clive Woodward says the key for him was to place a time limit on meetings. 'I tried to say at one point that no meeting should last longer than 30 minutes but that was a bit difficult,' he says. 'These days I say an hour but if we can finish within that time, we will. Keep the clock ticking. It's like a rugby game – there's a start and a finish.'

Nasser Hussain warns, though, that in a claustrophobic and competitive environment like professional sport, too many meetings between captain and coach can create a toxic atmosphere. 'I've never been one to have a meeting just for the sake of it,' he says. 'Everyone always has their eye on the captain and coach and they are always wondering if you are discussing them. There are so many insecurities at that high level. I know because towards the end of my playing career I was constantly looking at [coach Duncan] Fletcher and [captain Michael] Vaughan for clues in the body language and wondering if they were going to drop me.'

CREATING SPACE TO THINK

How leaders create space and time for themselves depends largely on their own personality and preferences. Charles Dunstone of the Carphone Warehouse, for instance, says that he does not consciously spend time mulling over problems, but trusts that the answer will eventually come. 'I find that our brains have a kind of simmering hotplate so if you have something that you're not sure about, don't fret about it too much and try not to consciously think about it. If you leave it for three days or so, the answer will come.' He adds that he is a natural observer, which is a rich source of ideas for the business. 'I go and look at other shops and read a lot. Ideas come from the most unlikely places. You just need to walk around in a state of readiness.' Dame Stella Rimington says that she made some of her best decisions while head of MI5 while she was walking her dogs: 'You're on your own and reasonably relaxed.'

Ron Dennis, the chairman of McLaren, tends to find comfort in order and neatness and says that a few hours spent putting his papers in order pays dividends in his intensely pressurized role. 'It's not unusual for me to wake at four in the morning and wrestle with a problem,' he says. 'What I tend to do is go downstairs, read a bunch of paperwork and make some notes, put it all in neat piles normally oriented at 90 degrees to each other in my briefcase, and then I'll feel fantastic about it. I might feel tired because I got up early but I know that I have hit the ground running and am on top of a whole range of issues that have cascaded onto me. I feel like I'm back in control. During the process the original problem that woke me becomes clearer and through my new found sense of order the solution materializes.'

Colonel Bob Stewart makes the point that the main task of a good leader is to make sound decisions, which means that they need to look after themselves when under pressure. 'The most important thing that a commander needs is sleep,' he says. 'Montgomery used to have eight hours sleep a night in a comfortable caravan because his logic was that his brain had to function well if he was going to save people's lives.' Colonel Stewart says he took the same approach wherever possible. 'I know that I need sleep so I used to break away from my responsibilities in order to get it. Practical leadership requires you to be in a position to make sound judgements.'

It is hardly surprising that the leaders with sporting backgrounds all turned to exercise as a means of escape and creating room for reflection. Sue Campbell, who is a former international netball player, says she will go and play a game of squash when she is facing a difficult decision: 'It never fails to work for me. I just relax.'

The former mid-distance runner Sebastian Coe, now head of the London Organising Committee for the Olympic and Paralympic Games, says that he could not function properly if he did not take regular exercise. 'I absolutely cling to the wreckage of exercise. It's the only thing that is never moved out of my diary. I did a two hour cycle ride at the weekend and probably at least an hour and a half was spent thinking about the week ahead. I can be tossing and turning over three or four things but when I go out for a run I can usually work it out and I wonder why I ever thought they were an issue in the first place.' He adds that his time as a politician taught him that rushed decisions are not always the best decisions, which is why taking time to exercise and reflect remains important to him:

'Sometimes at the end of a busy day you can be absolutely fixed on one course of action, but that would be the wrong decision because of the nature of the day on which the decision was made. It's a good lesson from politics that if you do something in a hurry you will often regret it the next day. I will occasionally go nuclear over something and fire off a letter but my secretary will put it in her desk until the next day, knowing that I might change my mind. Sometimes you just need that firebreak.'

For sporting leaders taking part in a pressurized competition, the best option is to take a step back from the game. The former England cricket captain Nasser Hussain says he used to lock himself away in his hotel room before a test match. 'I needed to give myself time to get my own game in order, so I would write things down, like my tactics for the game, or how I would bat against a particular bowler. I also used to walk around the streets, thinking about what the atmosphere would be like at Lords the next day.'

Like other sporting leaders, Hussain also turned to family and friends in the run-up to a big game. 'It's difficult to switch off as captain because people are constantly ringing you up for something. You need perspective and balance and family help with that. People within the game will tell you what you want to hear so you need a different angle.'

In the run-up to the rugby World Cup final, the England team spent time relaxing with their families in and around the team hotel, while the atmosphere whipped into a frenzy around them. The team's captain Martin Johnson says that the team were, in many ways, at their most relaxed in the days before the final:

> 'It was the biggest game of our lives and everyone knew that, so there was no point in panicking. We had to try and relax. We went training on the Tuesday before the final and hundreds of people turned up to watch. When we walked through the lobby of our hotel, which had a marble floor, the noise just rebounded everywhere. I just wanted to tell people to calm down. For me, the last week of the World Cup was the most relaxed of the whole tournament. We didn't want to increase the training at that stage so we did less training than we had done through the rest of our time out there.'

The question of maintaining some form of work-life balance is an issue for many of the leaders who are still involved in high-pressure organizations. Martin Glenn, for instance, says that he has become more confident in attempting to balance his life over recent years. 'I know I will work hard during the week but if one of my children has a school event, I will book that in. and I try to keep weekends as clear as I can.'

Kevin Roberts of Saatchi & Saatchi seems, on paper at least, to have a high-pressure existence, simply in terms of the amount of travel he undertakes as worldwide CEO of the company. His view, though, is that the work-life balance is a misleading term: 'It implies compromise and I don't think any of us want to live our lives in a compromised way any more.' Roberts' answer is to organize his working life so it is as stimulating and enjoyable as every other area of his life:

> *'I try to live and work in a completely integrated way so that my work is fantastic and my life is fantastic. The key is not to do anything that you don't like. I learned that from the age of 19. I don't do client dinners, even now. I will have a client meeting or a social dinner, but a business dinner is no fun, so I don't do it. After running a public company and talking to investors and analysts I couldn't do it anymore, so I hired a chairman to do it instead. I wouldn't necessarily recommend it as an approach to anyone else, but it is a way of handling work/life integration.'*

SELF-IMPROVEMENT AND LEARNING

The leaders we spoke to recognize the importance of maintaining their skills and 'edge' and many were keen to continue learning and gathering new experiences. Very few, however, took a formalized approach to continued self-improvement. Surprisingly, given his unorthodox approach to management, Greg Dyke is one of the few leaders in our sample (outside of the military leaders, who underwent formal training of their own) who have attended an academically-based leadership and management course, in Dyke's case at Harvard.

Gail Rebuck of Random House is another leader who has chosen to attend formal business training during her career. She says she is a great believer in personal renewal. 'Sometimes you can look at the year ahead and think, it's just another year, same old problems.

If you feel deflated then you can be sure that your staff will feel the same. I always say that my job is to keep a whole bank of light bulbs shining brightly at the same time, not flickering.' Rebuck says that she kept her own light shining brightly by taking a five week course at the Wharton business school at the University of Pennsylvania. 'I was a bit concerned that I was too old for it but I was feeling stale. I did come back with a new perspective fully renewed and a conviction that I had not spent enough time on training myself in the past, or the rest of the leadership team. We have introduced much better leadership training since then and it has really paid off'.'

Even so, all of the leaders showed a willingness to learn from new experiences and sometimes from unexpected sources. Sir Clive Woodward is one of the few to show a keen interest in management techniques, theories and publications, but says that some of the most important skills he learned during his time as coach to the England team came from a session the team spent with the Royal Marines:

> *'I learned a lot from the way the Marines approach leadership. The people we worked with made the point that when they jump out of a helicopter in Iraq or wherever they are, they have no idea what is going to happen. War is not a perfect business. Their view was that war was a series of cock-ups, and so that is what they train for. They can think they know what will happen but what they have to do is react to what actually happens. And their aim is to get back on the helicopter alive. It doesn't matter how you do it, you just have to do it. That was a brilliant lesson for me. You can have a great coach and a great team and the opposition can still outsmart you tactically on the pitch. You have to react to what they do during the game.'*

Woodward believes strongly in bringing experiences and skills from outside sport when working with players. 'I think I've been lucky in that I have worked in business and in sport,' he says. 'I encourage sports coaches to read business books and I like to find business mentors to come in and work with the team. I think that if you are a sports coach that has never worked outside of the sport and don't look for that input, you are on dangerous ground.'

RECOMMENDED READING

It is striking that many of the leaders we spoke to have a distrust – and in a couple of cases, an almost pathological dislike – of academic leadership and management literature. Charles Dunstone of the Carphone Warehouse says he has 'millions' of management books on his shelf, but confesses to having read only a few. 'I don't feel that I can change myself by reading a book,' he says. 'However much I think to myself, "I want to be more like that", you are who you are and I think it's quite difficult to change.'

'I'm always struck by the huge gap between many of the books and practice,' says Heather Rabbatts. 'I think Charles Handy is very intuitive about human behaviour but many management books I just refuse to read.' Rabbatts and Dunstone are not unusual among the leaders in saying that they prefer to read biographies of businesses and leaders and gathers valuable information from more narrative sources. 'I don't want to read a lot of management or leadership books but if I have the chance to go to a lecture, I will,' says Greg Dyke. 'I'd much rather meet someone who gives me the whole synopsis in 10 minutes. I'm a journalist and the whole art of journalism is to realize that the person in front of you knows a lot more about the subject than you do and so you pick their brains.'

'I like to read historical books [about leaders],' says Lord Inge. 'What made Peel such a successful prime minister? Why was Churchill so successful? It comes back to us all needing heroes.' Sue Campbell has the same view and has also read biographies of Churchill and Martin Luther King. 'I'm into heroes,' she says. 'They are not people you would necessarily want to be like, but you do get a sense of their immense commitment to a vision or a destiny. I've read Nelson Mandela's book and what a remarkable piece of leadership that was. It goes against everything you think leadership is because he wasn't there, making it happen, he was locked away from everyone. But he led a nation based on his values. That's leadership, isn't it?'

Nasser Hussain says that one of the most valuable books he has read is *The Art of Captaincy*, by the former England cricket captain Mike Brearley. 'I learned a lot about man management skills from that, in how he dealt with people like Ian Botham and got the best out of them. It was also really interesting about what being a captain was all about. The lines he wrote about when he retired as captain really helped me to prepare for my last week in the job.'

A number of the leaders have read management books that they have found useful and would recommend to others:

- *Reach for the Summit*, by Pat Head Summitt, an American basketball coach (recommended by Sue Campbell, who says it is an 'awesome book in terms of its application to management');
- *Good to Great* by Jim Collins (recommended by both Sir Clive Woodward and Martin Glenn);
- *Who Says Elephants Can't Dance? How I turned around IBM*, by Louis Gerstner (recommended by Woodward);
- *Winning* by Jack Welch (recommended by Woodward);
- *Geeks and Geezers: How Era, Values and Defining Moments Shape Leaders*, by Warren Bennis and Robert J Thomas (Recommended by Martin Glenn);
- *Execution: The Discipline of Getting Things Done* by Larry Bossidy, Ram Charan, Charles Buck and Clare Smith (recommended by Glenn); and
- *SUMO (Shut Up and Move On): The straight-talking guide to creating and enjoying a brilliant life*, by Paul McGee (recommended by Woodward).

LEADERSHIP AND LIFELONG LEARNING

In his book *Leading Change*, John Kotter says that his years of observation of leaders in various fields has led him to believe that the element that sets a leader apart, particularly in the modern business world that is characterized by dynamic, adaptive organizations, is their ability to continuously learn and develop.[1] As the environment in which people operate has changed and continues to do so, he argues, the willingness and ability of people to keep developing has become central to career success, just as the willingness for organizations to adapt and develop is central to economic success.

Kotter says that his study of students from Harvard Business School suggest that there were two key elements that gave some students an edge as their career progressed over the years – competitive drive and lifelong learning. The two are closely linked in that competitive drive helped to create lifelong learning, and together they help to produce an ability to cope with a fast-moving environment.

Kotter believes that individuals who demonstrate a willingness to be lifelong learners show a number of shared characteristics that, if the conditions are right, contribute to their achieving a leadership role. While bad luck can hit anyone during their career, lifelong learners show an ability to assess their mistakes as honestly as their successes, to work through the difficult times and to treat any setbacks as opportunities to learn. These individuals tend to take an open-minded approach to life and are particularly open to trying new ideas and taking risks. They are also natural observers of others and often go out of their way to seek new opinions and ideas from a wide range of sources.

The leaders contained in this book undoubtedly fit many of the characteristics identified by Kotter. They observed leadership traits in others as they grew up and during their early career, and tried to emulate what they saw as the most attractive attributes in their own leadership style. They tend to have a high degree of self-awareness and show an ability to analyse and assess their mistakes as well as their successes, and a willingness to learn from both. They are willing to take calculated risks and step outside their comfort zone, and are open to new ideas. They have high standards and expect the same from others, set ambitious but achievable goals and above all, have an intense passion for what they do.

Many of these leaders show additional abilities, most importantly a capacity to empathize with and understand the people they lead. They lead by persuasion, not by instruction. They select the people around them carefully and, once a mutually trusting relationship has developed, delegate decision-making downwards wherever possible. They welcome opinion and discussion. They do not expect unquestioning deference. And they seek to earn respect, rather than demand it.

This array of what are often called 'soft skills', however, does not mean that the leaders themselves are soft or forgiving. Rob Goffee and Gareth Jones characterize the empathetic skills shown by inspirational leaders as 'tough empathy', which effectively means giving followers what they need and not necessarily what they want.[2] 'Tough empathy,' say Goffee and Jones, 'balances respect for the individual and for the task at hand.'

As Goffee and Jones argue, empathy tends to be a natural characteristic of someone's personality and cannot be successfully faked. 'Real leaders don't need a training programme to convince their employees that they care,' they say. 'Real leaders empathize fiercely with the people they lead. They also care intensely about the work their employees do.'

Neither, would we say, can successful leadership be counterfeited. The leaders we spoke to were remarkably different people who operated under a wide range of contrasting conditions. Each had a distinctive leadership style that was largely dictated by their own skills and personality. Each had found a way that worked for them. They were and are, in Goffee and Jones' language, authentic leaders who had learned to be themselves, with skill. 'The key element is "with skill" and that is much harder than it looks,' Dr Gareth Jones told us. 'Successful leaders work hard at developing their leadership skills.'

KNOWING WHEN TO QUIT

Perhaps the most painful aspect of self-knowledge in a leader is knowing when the time is right to move on from the organization you lead. It is also, in many ways, the most valuable. History is littered with leaders, particularly political leaders, who failed to recognize that it was the right time to leave, with their dignity and reputation still intact.

The Mo Ibrahim Prize for Achievement in African Leadership, which was launched in London in 2006, is an interesting variation on this point. The annual award is the brainchild of telecommunications billionaire Mo Ibrahim and offers the winning leaders, who will have demonstrated that they can deliver security, educational and economic development to their constituents, $5m over 10 years once they leave office, plus $200,000 a year for life. Ibrahim believes that the financial trappings of senior office encourage corruption and hopes that the award will encourage leaders to become less passionate about clinging to office. 'Suddenly all the mansions, cars, food and wine are withdrawn,' Ibrahim told the *Financial Times*. 'Some find it difficult to rent a house in the capital. That incites corruption; it incites people to cling to office.'

The end of a leader's career with an organization is not always, of course, a matter of personal choice. Greg Dyke's resignation from the BBC in the wake of the Hutton Inquiry shows clearly that events can overtake the leader of an organization of any size. On the day that Dyke resigned, thousands of BBC staff walked out in protest and they later paid for a full-page advertisement in the *Daily Telegraph* in support of their director-general. As far as his employees were concerned, the time was clearly not right for Dyke to leave the organization. Dyke says in his autobiography *Inside Story* that 'the street protests weren't really about me. In the eyes of the staff, I represented the changes that [the culture change programme] *Making It Happen* had already brought about in the organization and their hopes for the future.'

For leaders with a free choice over their departure, though, the challenge is to recognize the point at which the organization is ready for a new leader. A number of the leaders we spoke to have shown an ability to recognize when the time is right to move on. Nasser Hussain says that the moment became clear to him while he was on the pitch with the rest of the England team, playing South Africa. 'It was bedlam around me and things just became clear. We were getting hammered and I looked around at the team and knew it was a team that no longer needed to be pushed but needed to be set in a different direction. I had got them as far as I could.'

Hussain adds that the reputation he had in the press for being a disciplinarian captain who brought pride and passion to the team contributed to his decision to resign. 'I started to believe my own press to some extent and looking back now I wish I hadn't at times because it's not the way to get the best out of people. You have to let people express themselves. It was the perfect progression for the team to move from me to [Michael] Vaughan because I had been cross and angry with the side for long enough. They needed a change of culture.'

The pressure of being captain as well as playing just under 100 test matches for England had also left him burnt out, he says. 'I was a different person at the end of it all than I was at the beginning, partly because I was a so-so player rather than a naturally talented one so I was constantly battling with myself. Someone once said that with my natural ability I should have played 60 or 70 test matches but I actually played 96. Those extra 20 or 30 games came because I was mentally tough and overcame my failings. But that makes you fragile over the years.'

The view of *The Times*' sports writer Simon Hughes was that Hussain was so effective as a captain because he was 'possessed by a demented ambition to end the endless years of disappointment and he took the job on with a searing fury. The furies exhausted him eventually and he resigned at the right moment, allowing Michael Vaughan to step in and lead with a relaxed air. It was time for the bad cop to go and the good cop to come in. Hussain's leadership was right for the time, Vaughan's for the time that followed. England were lucky with both, but luckier still with the transition from one to the other.'[4]

Heather Rabbatts also recognized when the time was right for her to move on from the London Borough of Lambeth: 'After three years with my senior team I knew they were the right people to take the organization to the next stage. I certainly knew at the end of my five years with Lambeth that I was not the right person to take it further forward. It's partly down to your own energy levels but also because you become captured by the organization that you have created. Instead of being in and against it, you are in and part of it.'

FINAL THOUGHTS ON LEADERSHIP

While our leaders acknowledge that leadership is a challenging, difficult and sometimes lonely job, one of the strongest messages to emerge was that all of them, irrespective of their field, took an enormous amount of pleasure from their role. 'I loved it,' says Lord Inge, who has now retired. 'More than I realized at the time, I think. Commanding your own regiment is something very special, when there are a lot of people involved and some of them have grown up with you.' Sir Clive Woodward says he also treasured his time as England coach. 'I loved it and when you're not in that type of role any more, you do miss it.' Martin Glenn adds that one of the most important things he got out of leadership was 'the warmth I got from the feeling that I had something worth saying.'

'The best thing I have ever done was to be captain of England,' says Nasser Hussain. 'And as Mike Brearley writes in his book, the difficult thing when you are not captain any more is not that the money is gone – it's that your team-mates don't call you Skip any more. Still, I have walked onto the pitch at Lord's while someone says over the tannoy that leading out England is Nasser Hussain. You can never take that away.'

As Hussain says, leadership can be enormously rewarding but it is also demanding and often involves a great deal of personal risk. Sebastian Coe tells of a conversation he had with a close friend soon after he was asked to lead the London 2012 Olympic and Paralympic Games Bid Committee:

> *'I said they had offered me the job, and what did he think. He looked at me and said, "It's a no-brainer, of course you have to take it." Then there was a short silence and he said, "Of course, if you f*** it up you won't be carrying the torch, you'll be carrying the can." And I thought yes, you are quite right.'*

Leaders are inevitably under the spotlight, whatever they do. When things go wrong, or equally when things go right, the responsibility ends with the leader. The ultimate test of any leader, though, is the state of the organization they leave behind at the end of their reign. Successful transformational leaders leave a lasting impression on the business – it is a different, better organization for having been led by them. The health and success of the organization is their legacy. In other words, the artist might get the attention, but it's the quality of the painting that matters.

[1] *Leading Change* p 178
[2] *Why Should Anyone Be Led by You?* Harvard Business Review, p68
[3] *Financial Times*, October 26, 2006
[4] *The Times*, March 24, 2006

Appendix

Some popular leadership theories and models

TRAIT THEORY

Trait theory first emerged in the early part of the 20th century and still forms the basis for anyone who believes that leaders are born and not made. Trait theory focuses entirely on the leader and the attributes and skills that make a leader and does not consider situational aspects or the leader's followers.

The first major study of leadership traits, by Stogdill in 1948, identified a number of traits that set a member of a group apart as a leader. These included: intelligence; insight; initiative; responsibility; persistence; sociability and self-confidence. A number of studies carried out since have helped to identify a longer list of traits most prevalent in leaders, although trait theory has faltered in general because no list that could be described as definitive could be agreed upon.

The common leadership traits recognized are:

- Adaptability to situations;
- Alertness to their social environment;
- Ambitiousness and achievement oriented;
- Assertiveness;
- Decisiveness;
- Dependability;
- A desire to influence others;
- High energy levels;
- Persistence;
- Self-confidence;
- Ability to cope with stress;
- Tendency towards supportiveness; and
- Willingness to assume responsibility.

SKILLS APPROACH

The skills approach to leadership theory again concentrates on the leader and not on situational aspects, but focuses on the skills and abilities that a leader needs, rather than the personality traits that he or she might have been born with.

The skills approach began in earnest with an article by Robert Katz in the Harvard Business Review in 1955, called *Skills of an Effective Administrator*. He suggested that effective leadership demanded three basic personal skills: technical skills (relating to their own specific field), human skills (the ability to work with people) and conceptual skills (the ability to work with ideas). This was developed further in the 1990s into the capability model of leadership, which identified five components of leadership performance: competency; individual attributes; leadership outcomes; social skills and knowledge. The model suggests that a leader's performance is set by his or her competencies, which are influenced in turn by the leader's experiences, attributes and the environment in which they operate.

ADAIR'S THREE CIRCLES APPROACH

John Adair developed the three circles approach to leadership at Sandhurst during the 1970s by observing what leaders did to gain the support of their followers. Adair suggested that effective leaders concentrate on three areas of need within a team: the needs relating to the task in hand (which would include setting a clear objective and managing the process); the needs relating to the team as a whole (such as effective teamworking, support and communication); and the needs relating to each individual member of the team. While the emphasis on each circle may vary, he argued, a leader should always be aware of all three:

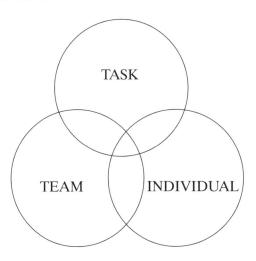

SITUATIONAL LEADERSHIP

The situational approach to leadership was developed in the 1960s by Paul Hersey and Ken Blanchard and concentrates on how leaders adapt their behaviour according to the situation they are in. The situational leadership model says that leadership has a directive and a supportive element and each has to be applied appropriately according to the situation. The approach is illustrated through the following grid:

+	SUPPORTING	COACHING
Supportive Behaviour		
	DELEGATING	DIRECTING
‒		

‒   Directive Behaviour   +

The grid classifies leadership style into four categories:

- *Directing approach* – the leader sets goals and tasks for the followers and focuses on communicating those goals and achieving them. There is less focus on supportive behaviour.
- *Coaching approach* – the leader sets tasks and goals but with input and discussion from followers. Communication is more two-way than in the directing approach, but the final decisions still rests with the leader.
- *Supporting approach* – the leader listens, asks for input and provides advice and feedback but delegates day-to-day decisions to the followers.
- *Delegating approach* – control is passed to the follower. The leader has less involvement in the planning of goals and once the direction is decided with the leader, the follower takes on responsibility for achievement.

CONTINGENCY THEORY

Developed by Fred Fielder in the 1960s, the contingency theory of leadership argues that effective leadership depends on finding the best way to manage in any given situation. Fielder argued that situations have three dimensions that can be used to assess the effectiveness of a leader:

- *Leader-member relations* – this includes the level of loyalty demonstrated towards the leader, the level of confidence in the leader displayed by followers, and the leader's overall attractiveness to followers.
- *Task structure* – the level to which tasks are specified, since the more structured the tasks, the greater control a leader has.
- *Position power* – the level of authority maintained by the leader, including the leader's ability to punish or reward followers.

The most favourable situations are defined as those that have good leader-member relations, clearly defined tasks and strong position power. Contingency theory argues that different leadership styles will be effective in different situations.

TRANSFORMATIONAL LEADERSHIP

Transformational leadership focuses on the ability of a leader to change their followers in ways that result in their being motivated to perform at a higher level than before. Transformational leaders are seen as inspirational and visionary with strong communication skills and a deep-rooted interest in people.

Transformational leaders concentrate on increasing their followers' awareness of the importance of their tasks and try to develop their desire to work for the good of the organization as a whole, rather than for their own personal gain. A study published in 1986 by Tichy and DeVanna identified a number of characteristics of transformational leaders:

- They recognize the need for change
- They have an ability to deal with complex situations and problems
- They adopt a values-driven approach and express strong ideals
- They are personally courageous
- They create coalitions of followers and a spirit of co-operation.

Transformational leadership is often contrasted with transactional leadership, where the leader–follower relationship is based on a straightforward exchange of work for pay and benefits.

Bibliography and Further Reading

Why Should Anyone Be Led By You? by Rob Goffee and Gareth Jones. Harvard Business School Press (Boston) 2006.

Why Should Anyone Be Led By You? by Rob Goffee and Gareth Jones. Harvard Business Review, September–October 2000 pp 61–71.

Leading Change by John P Kotter. Harvard Business School Press (Boston) 1996

What Leaders Really Do by John P Kotter. Breakthrough Leadership, Harvard Business Review, December 2001 pp 85–97.

Sea Harrier Over The Falklands by Commander 'Sharkey' Ward. Cassell Military Paperbacks (London) 2000.

In the Eye of the Storm by Major General Patrick Cordingley. Hodder and Stoughton (London) 1996

Inside Story by Greg Dyke. HarperCollins (London) 2004.

Martin Johnson: The Autobiography. Headline Book Publishing (London) 2004.

Open Secret: The Autobiography of the former Director-General of MI5 by Stella Rimington. Arrow Books (London) 2002.

Playing with Fire by Nasser Hussain. Penguin Books (London) 2005.

Winning! The Story of England's Rise to World Cup Glory by Clive Woodward. Hodder & Stoughton (London) 2004.

29 Leadership Secrets from Jack Welch by Robert Slater. McGraw-Hill (New York) 2003.

Leadership Theory and Practice by Peter G Northouse. Sage Publications (Thousand Oaks, California) 2004.

The Secrets of Great Groups by Warren Bennis. Leader to Leader 3 (Winter 1997) 29–33

Defeat Into Victory: Battling Japan in Burma and India by Field-Marshal Viscount Slim. Cooper Square Press (New York) 2000.

Index